Cushions

Contents

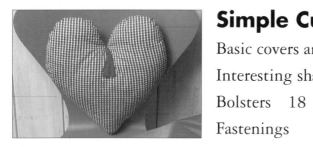

Floor and Seating Cushions   56

Hand-Stitched Cushions   66

Sewing Techniques   80

Very easy

A little skill

Some experience

Before you Begin

Cushions are usually the final addition to a room's decor, but before you just run up a couple of plain, square covers, think about how your whole scheme could be transformed by using a bit of imagination.

Mix and match interesting shapes and unusual fabrics – with scatter cushions, for example, you can use dressmaking fabrics rather than soft furnishing material, because they don't have to put up with much wear and tear. Different fillings give you further options. Choose from a range that includes solid foam for cushions that need to fit into shaped seats, and soft feathers for those that are tossed onto beds or sofas. But whatever type of cushions you decide to make, the most important thing is to remember that they can be made in just about any form you like – and then enjoy discovering how creative you can be.

Fabric colours and designs

Taking a little care over how you choose your colours and designs will make a huge difference. When it comes to thinking about colour schemes for your cushions, there are just a few simple principles to bear in mind. Remember that even the smallest cushions can still have a strong colour influence on a room. See just how much a group of brightly-coloured cushions can relieve a large neutral area, or how a range of subtle cushions will tone down and harmonise the most exuberant interior.

MIXING AND MATCHING

▼► Never be afraid of using colour. It's not difficult to mix and match different shades together and, by following a few straightforward rules, you will find yourself creating some delightful decorative schemes. It will help greatly if you group different colours in some way. The simplest approach is to divide colours into two basic categories – neutral shades and true colours.

WORKING WITH NEUTRAL SHADES

▲ Neutral shades are often the basis for a pale and interesting but restrained room. Add a touch of life by using textured fabrics – from subtle sheens to knobbly and heavily woven fabrics.

WORKING WITH TRUE COLOURS

◀ Closely related, harmonious colours will provide an easy-to-live-with cushion selection. To create successful schemes, bear in mind the arrangement of colours known as the colour wheel. Like the rainbow, this wheel is made up of red, orange, yellow, green, blue and violet.

◀ Contrasting colours lie directly opposite each other on the wheel, adding accents of contrasting colour with scatter cushions could bring your decor to life; even contrasting frill or piping can lift your colour scheme.

Look closely at different patterned fabrics to see how designers use contrasting colours to breathe life into a particular design. Fabric collections often have designs in bright tones of harmonious shades and then one or two designs with contrasting touches.

MAKING YOUR CHOICE

Once you have decided on the shades you prefer, take your favourite colour samples to the shops. Before you begin to choose fabrics for your cushions, collect small samples in colours and designs that appeal to you, take them home and see for yourself just how certain combinations will work together. Or you can simply buy enough to make up one small cushion cover, and leave it lying in the room over the sofa or chair to gauge how the fabric looks in sunlight and in artificial light. Once you have settled on a suitable colour scheme, you can move on and work out the shape and style of the cushions that will enhance your particular scheme even more (see pages 8–9).

DESIGN MOTIFS

Patterns should generally be centred on cushion fronts and backs and matched so that they meet at the side seams, unless the edge is broken up with a frill or edging such as piping. Be wary of large motifs in patterned fabric, unless you are making extra-large cushions.

HOT AND COLD

▼ Colours can also be divided into hot colours, such as red, orange and yellow, and cool colours – green, blue and violet. In-between are the warm and cooler shades.

▼ Think about using cushions to alter the 'climate' of a room. Try hot-coloured cushions to add warmth in cold, north-facing rooms, or to make a room more restful use cool colours in simple shapes.

Shapes and styles

Before you decide on the shape and style of your cushions you must take three important things into consideration. First, think about the style and design of your flat or house. Secondly, consider the style of the rest of the furnishings. Thirdly, think carefully about your reasons for adding cushions. For guidance, look through magazines to see how to use cushions as style pointers in different rooms.

STYLE POINTERS

CONTRASTS

▲ Different shapes and styles can look very dramatic when placed together in a room, but it may take considerable confidence and practice to achieve this with real flair and panache. You might want to start out with more modest experiments, such as adding unusual trims.

▲ As a general principle, cool, modern interiors with minimalist-style furniture are enhanced by smaller cushions in clean-cut shapes, made from crisp, cool linens or well-pressed, sleek, semi-textured fabrics. Grander decor, however, will benefit from larger-scale, more opulent designs.

ON THE RIGHT SCALE

◀ Dimension is an important factor when fitting cushions into a decor – overcrowding sofas and chairs with larger-than-life cushions will only reduce the seating space, while tiny, delicate cushions on large, streamlined sofas will look totally out of proportion. Try making up a series of pads before you cut out the main fabric and leave them scattered in the areas you wish to dress – you'll soon know where cushions will be best employed and which size will be the most comfortable.

STYLED THEMES

▲ For oriental schemes, arrange cushions featuring one-colour prints against an open, spacious furnishing background with uncluttered lines. Really brightly coloured decors are usually at home with any shape and size of cushion, as long as it is dressed up in an eye-catching print.

TAKING SHAPE

▲ Try experimenting with different shapes. It can be fun to make up your own, and as long as the outline is not too complicated, it is easy to achieve a good result. Simply enlarge your design outline on a photocopier and cut this out twice in fabric. Add gussets to give depth to cushion shapes and for cushions used to pad seats and benches.

Fabric types, pads and fillings

Covers can be made up in almost any fabric, but it is logical to avoid certain types, such as very fine or loosely-woven materials. Cushion covers generally need frequent laundering, and the best fabrics to use from this point of view often belong to the cotton-based families. For cushions that can be used all round the house, choose tough, hard-wearing fabrics – closely-woven cottons, linens and cotton polyester mixes are good bets. Avoid bulky fabrics that are difficult to sew or need specialist pressing.

EXCEPTIONS TO THE RULE

Tough cottons or cotton-synthetic mixes may be especially good choices, but you will probably want more leeway than this. If you must use flimsy fabric, try fixing it to a backing of plain, fine cotton. Totally synthetic fabrics, such as the glitzy, metallic materials, aren't always wonderful from the washing point of view, but they may be just the thing to liven up your decor – and are best used on the small surface area of a cushion. Similarly, small, precious oddments of fabric that you've collected or bought at sales may be perfect for cushions – they would probably be impractical or too expensive to use over any larger area.

NATURAL OR MAN-MADE?

Fibres used in home furnishing fabrics generally fall into two categories – natural and man-made. Natural fibres such as wool, linen, cotton and silk clean well, although they can shrink and crease badly. Man-made fabrics may not have such a good appearance, but they often wash well, keep their shape and are crease-resistant, especially those derived from natural materials, such as rayon and viscose. However, manufacturers have now combined natural fibres with man-made ones to bring mixes that offer the best of both worlds.

CUSHION PADS

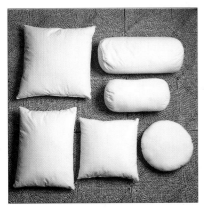

Cushions need a substantial pad to prolong their life and maintain their shape. Choose your style, shape and outer fabric then consider the pad.

There is a good range of cushion pads available on the market in a range of popular shapes. They come in a wide selection of sizes – square pads, for example, range from 30cm (12in) up to 91cm (36in).

If you are making a cushion in an odd size, or want to use a particular filling, then making up your own pad is definitely the answer. Pad covers can be made from a variety of inexpensive fabrics, such as calico, ticking or lining fabric. For a long life, choose hard-wearing, firmly-woven cotton. Feather-filled pads must be made from a downproof fabric with a waxed reverse side, so that the feathers won't work their way through the fabric.

CUSHION FILLINGS

When choosing your filling, bear in mind the position of the cushion and how much wear it should expect. The different types are:

Feathers

This is the traditional filling for cushions. Feathers are often mixed with down which gives a soft, luxurious cushion needing only a quick shake to retain the shape.

Kapok

This is a soft and inexpensive vegetable filling, often used in the past for cushions. Pads stuffed with Kapok will eventually lose their shape.

Synthetic fibres

These fillings are inexpensive, washable and hypo-allergenic, and can be covered with cotton or calico. They come packed in bags or in sheets of wadding, in various thicknesses.

Foam

Foam is available as chips, shredded or in blocks and is a particularly good choice for garden cushions. Foam chips and shredded foam provide cheap, non-absorbent fillings, but they can be lumpy, so wrap the pad in a layer of wadding to smooth the outline before fitting it inside the cover. Block foam is ideal for boxy shapes, but is hard to shape correctly yourself, so get your supplier to cut the foam to the correct size for you – you can even take a template to the shop for the supplier to cut round.

Polystyrene granules

Small, expanded polystyrene beads form a good filling for floor cushions and children's cushions as it makes the cushions light to lift. The beads move about and so mould to the contours of the sitter, producing a comfortable seat – ideal for the many younger people who prefer the floor to sitting on a sofa.

Simple Cushions

Sofas piled high with simple cushions in an assortment of different colours and patterns always look inviting. Basic cushion covers are quick and easy to make and use a minimum of fabric. Try co-ordinating them with existing furnishings by using fabric left over from loose covers or curtains. Or make them from small, treasured pieces of fabric.

If you want a change from square and rectangular outlines, you'll find that round cushions are quick to make, while hearts, triangles and letters add interest and fun, and easy-to-make bolsters supply an elegant, tailored touch. You also have a choice when it comes to fastening methods. Choose straightforward closures such as slipstitching, vents and ties or for a discreet finish use zips or Velcro.

Basic covers and pads

Basic cushion covers are simply a fabric shape with a slipstitch opening placed centrally in one edge. As for cushion pads, these are readily available in a good selection of sizes, but by producing your own you can make non-standard size cushions – for example, if you are using an unusually small fabric off-cut for your cover. To make the cushion pad choose down-proof ticking, cambric, calico, curtain lining, sheeting or a similar closely-woven cotton fabric.

MATERIALS: *Basic square cushion cover, 40cm (16in) square:* 46cm (½yd) of furnishing fabric, 140cm (55in) wide; same-size cushion pad, matching thread, tape measure, scissors, pins and needles
Basic square cushion pad, 40cm (16in) square: 46cm (½yd) of fabric, 90cm (36in) wide, suitable for chosen filling (feathers or polyester); matching thread, tape measure, scissors, pins and needles

FABRIC: (Cushion and pad): *Front and back:* two squares of fabric, 3cm (1¼in) larger than the desired cushion size

BASIC SQUARE COVER

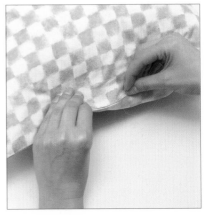

1 Place cushion back and front pieces with right sides together and matching raw edges. Pin, tack and stitch the two pieces together round four corners and three sides, leaving an opening centrally in the remaining side. Work a few backstitches at the beginning and end of the seam to secure the stitches.

2 Trim the corners diagonally, 3mm (⅛in) from the stitching. For the opening, fold the seam allowance under and press edges flat and the seams open. Turn the cover right side out, pulling out the corners. Press the cover flat, with the seams right at the very edge of the cover.

3 Insert the cushion pad. Pin the cover opening together and use slipstitch to close it. Make up rectangular covers (and pads) in the same way as square covers, positioning the opening centrally in one short side. For a cushion 46 x 36cm (18 x 14in), you will need 46cm (½yd) of 140cm (55in) wide fabric.

CUSHION PADS

Make up a cushion pad in the same way as a cover, leaving an opening in one side. Insert the filling by using a large-gauge knitting needle or wooden spoon handle to work it well into the corners. Instead of slipstitching the opening closed, machine stitch it, to hold the filling firmly in place.

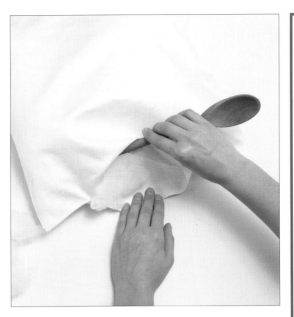

TIDY CORNERS

To eliminate wrinkled corners on plain square and rectangular cushion covers, sew round the corners in a curve. The degree of the curve will depend on the size of the cover.

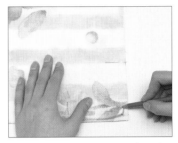

1 Fold the piece of fabric for the front cover in half both ways. Mark halfway between the fold and the corner on each open side. Mark 1.5cm (⅝in) in from the corner point. Now draw a line round the corner in a gentle curve, from the centre marks through the corner mark.

2 Keeping the cover folded, cut along the marked line. Use the front as a pattern to cut out the back cover. Now make up the cushion cover in the usual way, as in steps 1-3 of the previous section.

Interesting shapes

Cushions can be made in any shape, provided the outline isn't too complicated. First, draw an outline of your shape, smoothing out any over-complicated areas. Use a photocopier to enlarge the design to the chosen size and check that the shape is still recognisable. Cut out the pattern. If it's an unusual shape, you will need to make your own pad. Do this first, as this will help you to check whether the pattern works.

MATERIALS: *Round cushion, 30cm (12in) in diameter:* 46cm (½yd) of furnishing fabric, 140cm (55in) wide; same-size cushion pad, matching thread, paper, pencil, string, drawing pin, large cork tile or clean wooden chopping board, tape measure, scissors, pins and needles
Heart-shaped cushion, approximately 38cm (15in) square: 46cm (½yd) of furnishing fabric, 90cm (36in) wide; same-size cushion pad, dressmakers' squared pattern paper and pencil, matching thread, tape measure, scissors, pins and needles

FABRIC: *Round cushion, front and back:* Measure the diameter of the pad and add 1.5cm (⅝in) seam allowance all round to give the size for the front and back
Heart-shaped cushion, front and back: Draw up a pattern (see step 1 right) and use this to cut two pieces from your fabric, adding 1.5cm (⅝in) seam allowance all round the outer edge

ROUND CUSHION COVER

1 To ensure a good result, make a paper pattern – cut a square of paper slightly larger than the cutting size of the circle. Fold in half both ways. Now cut a length of string about 20cm (8in) longer than half the radius of the circle. Tie one end round the pointed end of a pencil. Push a drawing pin through the opposite end so that the distance between the two equals half the radius of the circle. Place the paper pattern on a cork tile or chopping board and anchor the drawing pin into the folded corner. Holding the string taut, draw across the paper from edge to edge.

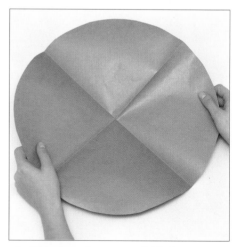

2 Keeping the paper folded, cut along the marked outline. Open out your paper. Use the pattern to cut out two cover pieces. If the fabric has a large motif, then centre this on both the front and back.

3 Place with right sides together and matching outer edges. Pin, tack and stitch two-thirds of the way round the outer edge, taking 1.5cm (⅝in) seam allowance. Work a few backstitches at either end of the seam to secure the stitches. Snip into the seam allowance at regular intervals round the circle.

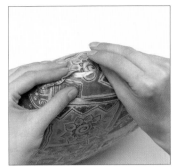

4 Turn the cover right side out. Press so that the seam is right at the outer edge. Press the seam allowance under along the opening. Insert cushion pad and slipstitch the open edges closed.

HEART-SHAPED CUSHION COVER

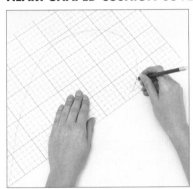

1 Cut a piece of pattern paper and fold in half lengthways. Draw half a heart pattern, using the fold of the paper as the heart's centre. Keeping the paper folded, cut out your outline. Unfold the paper and check the shape and size. Alter as necessary.

2 Use your pattern to cut out a cushion front and back, adding 1.5cm (⅝in) seam allowance. Place pieces with right sides together and matching outer edges. Pin, tack and stitch together, leaving an opening at the base of one side edge. Work a few backstitches at the beginning and end of the seam to secure the stitches.

3 Cut into the seam allowance round the edges and turn the cover right side out. Press the seam allowance under on either side of the opening and press the seam along the outer edge. Make up a pad and insert. Slipstitch the open edges together and add decorations, such as the tassel shown here, if desired.

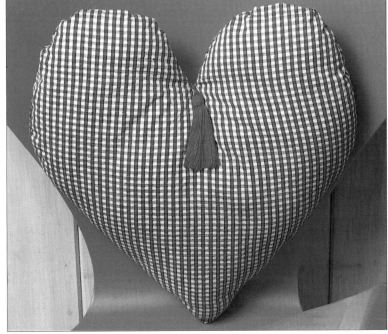

Bolsters

Bolsters have crisp edges and a long opening in the seam on the centre section, making the covers easy to remove for cleaning. Choose between a gathered style – where the ends are gathered up and disguised by a large, self-covered button – or a neat tailored look. Ready-made bolster pads come in a good range of sizes, or make your own by following the instructions for the tailored bolster but machine-stitch the opening closed after the filling has been added. The opening can be slipstitched or closed with a zip (see pages 20–21).

MATERIALS: *Gathered bolster, 46cm (18in) long, with 18cm (7in) diameter ends:* 46cm (½yd) of furnishing fabric, 140cm (55in) wide; same-size bolster pad, two self-covering buttons, 3.5cm (1½in) in diameter and a small amount of contrast fabric for covering, matching thread, tape measure, scissors, pins and needles
Tailored bolster of the same size: 46cm (½yd) of furnishing fabric, 140cm (55in) wide; same-size bolster pad, matching thread, tape measure, scissors, pins and needles, paper and pair of compasses for pattern

FABRIC: *Gathered bolster, length:* Measure the length of the pad from seam to seam. Measure across the end. Add both measurements together and add 3cm (1¼in) seam allowances
Depth: Measure round the pad and add 3cm (1¼in) seam allowances. Cut out one rectangle of fabric to this size
Tailored bolster, centre section: Measure the length of the pad and add 3cm (1¼in) seam allowances. Measure the pad's circumference and add the seam allowance. Cut one rectangle of fabric to this size
Ends: Measure the diameter of one end of the bolster pad and divide by two. On a sheet of paper, draw a circle with the compasses set to this measurement. Cut out the pattern and use to cut out the ends

GATHERED BOLSTER

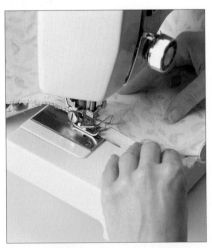

1 Fold fabric in half lengthways, with right sides together and matching raw edges. Pin, tack and stitch into a cylinder shape, taking 1.5cm (⅝in) seam allowance. Neaten both raw edges with zigzag stitch and press seam open.

2 Turn the cover the right way round. Fold over raw edges at each end by 1.5cm (⅝in). Using a double thread, work large, evenly-spaced gathering hand stitches round each turned-over edge; leave the gathering thread threaded on a needle.

3 Insert the bolster pad, centring it inside the cover and matching pad and cover seams. At each end, pull up the gathering threads to close the end and fasten off the thread.

4 Cover each button mould with contrasting or matching fabric, (see Covering Buttons). Hand-stitch the covered button over each gathered-up end to neaten.

TAILORED BOLSTER

1 Fold centre section over, with right sides together and matching raw edges. Pin, tack and stitch, taking 1.5cm (⅝in) seam allowance and leaving a central opening; which you may want to close with a zip (see pages 20–21). Snip into the seam allowance round each end of the centre section.

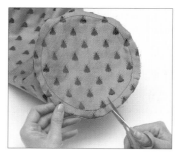

2 Open the zip (if necessary). With right sides together, pin, tack and stitch an end circle into each end of the centre section. Snip into the seam allowance and trim the seams. Turn cover right side out, insert pad and close the opening. Piping cord will define the tailored edges (see pages 32–33).

COVERING BUTTONS

Follow the manufacturer's instructions for covering buttons. Use a guide to cut a circle of your chosen fabric. Run a gathering thread round the outer edge and gather the covering around the button mould, fasten off. Ease the fabric evenly round the outer edge of the mould and snap fit the button back.

Fastenings

Place cover openings along one edge or vertically or horizontally across the back. Simple ways of fastening them closed include slipstitching the opening, forming an overlapping vent, or making an envelope-style opening that is closed with ties or buttons. More complicated options are zips and Velcro. Lapped zips are placed in one edge of the cover, preferably the base edge, while those inserted across the back can be placed centrally or lower down. With Velcro, stop the stitches from showing on the right side by using a double hem on the edges of the opening and stitching the Velcro to that (don't forget to add extra fabric on these edges to allow for this double hem). Measure the tape width and allow twice this for the hem. With Velcro spots or tape, use 1.5cm (⅝in) wide hems.

OVERLAPPING VENT

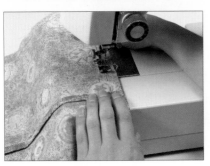

1 Cut out the cushion back, making it 11.5cm (4½in) wider than the front and so allowing for a 7cm (2¾in) overlap at the back of the cushion. Fold the back in half and cut along the fold. Fold under a double 1cm (⅜in) hem down the centre back edges of each back section and press firmly. Pin, tack and stitch the hems.

2 Place cushion backs with right sides up, overlapping the centre hem edges by 7cm (2¾in). Using diagonal stitches, tack the centre edges together.

3 Place the back and front together, with right sides facing and matching outer edges. Pin, tack and stitch all round. Trim, turn right side out and insert pad.

CENTRAL ZIP

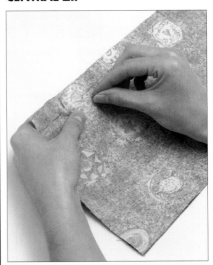

1 Choose a zip 5–10cm (2–4in) shorter than the cushion width. Place the two back cover pieces with right sides together and raw edges matching. Pin and tack together along the centre edge, taking 1.5cm (⅝in) seam allowance. Mark the zip length centrally across the tacked seam. Stitch from each side, up to the marks, working a few backstitches at each side to fasten. Press seam open.

2 With the right sides of the fabric down, place the zip, also right side down, over the seam. Position the teeth centrally, over the tacked section of the seam. Pin and tack in place.

3 Turn the back over and stitch all round the zip. Snip away the tacking threads and open zip. Complete the cover in the usual way.

LAPPED ZIP

1 Pick a zip 5–10cm (2–4in) shorter than the cushion side edge. Place back and front pieces, right sides together and matching raw edges. Pin and tack across the side seam. Mark the zip length centrally on the tacked seam. Stitch in from each side, up to the marks, leaving 1.5cm (⅝in) seam allowance. Work a few backstitches to fasten. Press the seam open.

2 Open the zip and place right side down on the front seam allowance only, with zip teeth against the seam-line; pin and tack. Using a zip foot, machine-stitch the zip to the seam allowance only.

3 Close the zip. Spread the cover flat, right sides up, covering the zip teeth with the back seam allowance. Pin, tack and stitch the zip in place 1.5cm (⅝in) from the seamline and across each end. Refold cover, right sides together and pin, tack and stitch the remaining three sides.

VELCRO TAPE

1 Turn under a double hem width on the opening edges of each piece; press and pin. Mark either end of the central opening with a pin.

2 Separate the two halves of the tape. Unfold the first fold of the hem and pin one piece of tape centrally over, through a double thickness of material. Pin and stitch the edges. Repeat, to stitch tape to the other cover piece. Check that the two halves will match when the cover is stitched together.

3 Refold the double hems and pin. Place the cover pieces right sides together and stitch in from each side edge to 1cm (⅜in) beyond the end of the fastening tape, alongside the hem edge. Work a few backstitches to fasten the stitches. Pin, tack and stitch the remaining three sides, catching in the folded hems.

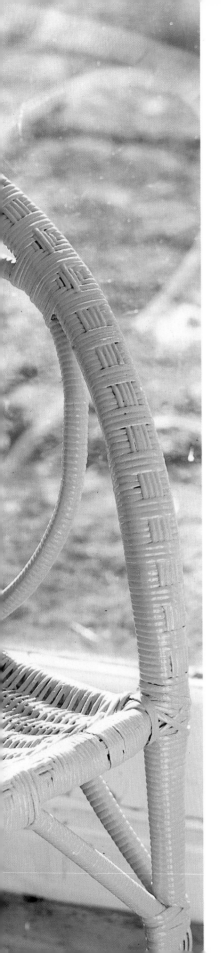

Decorative Finishes

Find the perfect match for your individual skills, schedule and sense of style by choosing from the huge variety of fastenings and decorative finishes – this is an area where you really can give your imagination free rein. A single border provides a distinctive edge, while double borders and frills are simple ways to create a really luxurious look. The plainest cover is transformed by adding piping round the edges, accentuating the outline and giving the cushion longer life, and the stunning range of braids, cords and trims on the market lend any cushions a touch of class. Decoration need not be fussy or complicated – simply making a feature of the way you fasten your cushion cover by using attractive ties and buttons is an easy and appealing option.

Borders

A border is simple and lends a special touch to your cushions. Single-bordered or 'flanged' cushions are stitched together before an integral border is formed by topstitching all round the outer edge. A double border gives a really luxurious look. The mitred double border is created on the front and back cushion pieces before they are stitched together.

MATERIALS: *40cm (16in) square cushion with a 6cm (2½in) wide single border:* 60cm (¾yd) of furnishing fabric, 140cm (55in) wide; 40cm (16in) square cushion pad, matching thread, tape measure, scissors, pins and needles
Same size cushion with a 5cm (2in) wide double border: 70cm (¾yd) of furnishing fabric, 140cm (55in) wide; same size cushion pad, matching thread, tape measure, scissors, pins and needles

FABRIC: *Cushion with 6cm (2½in) single border, front and back:* Measure pad width and length, adding twice the width of the border plus 3cm (1¼in) seam allowance to each measurement
Cushion with 5cm (2in) double border, front: Measure the pad width and length and add an extra 23cm (9in) to both measurements for the border and outer seam allowance
Back: Cut one piece of fabric to the same size as the front, adding an extra 3cm (1¼in) seam allowance to one measurement for a central opening

SINGLE BORDER

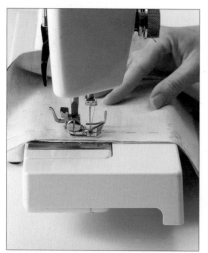

1 Place front and back cover pieces right sides together and matching raw edges. Pin, tack and stitch, leaving a space for the opening. Turn cover right side out and press the seams.

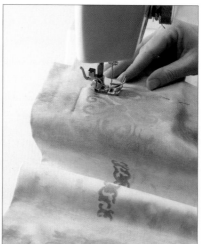

2 Pin and machine-stitch round the cover again at the chosen border width, leaving a gap in the stitching at the main opening.

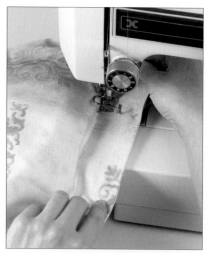

3 Insert the pad. Pin and tack the opening closed. Using a piping foot stitch across the inner gap, matching up with the previous stitching. Slipstitch the outer opening closed.

DOUBLE BORDER

1 If desired, insert a fastening in a central back seam or form a central opening that can be slipstitched. Lay the back cover piece flat, wrong side up. On all four sides, fold over the border width plus 1.5cm (⅝in) seam allowance. Press firmly. Repeat for the front cover.

2 Open out the folded border and press in each corner until the pressed lines at a corner match the pressed lines along edges of cover. Press the diagonal fold.

3 Open out the first corner. With right sides together, fold the corner in half diagonally, matching the outer edges. Stitch across the corner along the pressed foldline, forming a mitred corner. Trim down the seam allowance. Press open. Repeat with each corner.

4 Turn each corner right side out and press flat. Repeat this to form similar corners on the front cover piece.

5 Place front and back pieces with wrong sides together, matching the mitred corners. Pin, tack and stitch the pieces together all round the cover, at your chosen border distance from the outer edge. Insert the pad and close the opening with slipstitch or a zip.

Fancy frills

Frilled cushions always look extravagant. A frill is usually one and a half times or twice the perimeter of the cushion, but this depends on the required fullness and the weight of the fabric – heavy fabric will not pull up neatly into tight frills. Frills are usually gathered, but they can also be pleated or gathered only at the corners. Single frills are generally cut on the straight of the grain, across the fabric width, and hemmed along one edge; a double frill is basically a strip of fabric folded in half to provide a more substantial border and it hangs better if cut on the fabric's bias.

MATERIALS: *38cm (15in) diameter round cushion with an 8cm (3in) wide single frill:* 70cm (¾yd) of furnishing fabric, 140cm (55in) wide; same-size cushion pad, matching thread, tape measure, scissors, pins and needles
46cm (18in) square cushion with a 10cm (4in) wide double frill 70cm (¾yd) of furnishing fabric, 140cm (55in) wide; same-size cushion pad, matching thread, tape measure, scissors, pins and needles

FABRIC: *Round cushion, front and back:* Measure across the pad and add 3cm (1¼in) seam allowance. Cut two circles of fabric (see pages 18–19). For a centre-back opening, use half the circular pattern, but with an extra 3cm (1¼in) added to the straight edge as a seam allowance
Frill: Measure the circumference of the pad and allow an extra 1½–2 times this length. Decide on the width of the frill and add 3.5cm (1½in) for hem and seam allowances. Cut strips across the width of your fabric which, when stitched together, come to the correct length
Square cushion, front and back: Measure the pad width and length and add 3cm (1¼in) seam allowance. Cut two pieces of fabric. For a centre-back opening, add an extra 3cm (1¼in) seam allowance to the width or length of the cushion back and cut the back into two equal pieces
Frill: Measure one edge of the pad and multiply by four, then multiply again by two. Decide on the width of your frill, then double this measurement and add 3cm (1¼in) seam allowance. Cut out fabric strips to the correct width on the bias of the fabric, so that, when stitched together, these form the correct length

SINGLE FRILL

1 Use French seams to join the frill strips together into a ring. Turn up the base edge to form a double 1cm (⅜in) hem, pin, tack and stitch.

2 Mark the edge of the front cover and the frill into equal sections. Machine stitch two rows of gathering stitches across each section of the frill.

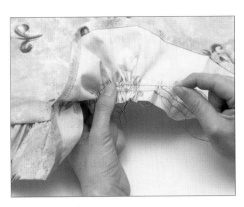

3 Match the sections of the frill to the sections on the cover, pulling up the gathers to fit. Pin, tack and stitch in place. Complete the cover as for a basic cover (see pages 14–17) or add a zip centre-back (see pages 20–21).

ADDING FRILLS TO SQUARE COVERS

To make a frill easier to add to a square cover, gently round off the corners of your cover pieces (try drawing your curved corner round an upside-down egg cup).

DOUBLE FRILL

1 Join the frill strips together into a ring with plain seams, taking 1.5cm (⅝in) seam allowance. Trim and press the seams open. Fold the frill in half with wrong sides together and matching raw edges.

2 As for the single-frilled cover, mark the frill and cover into sections, gather up the frill and stitch to the front cover piece and complete the cover.

3 On square and rectangular covers, allow extra gathers round each corner, so that, when the cover is turned right side out, the frill will look full at each corner, and not strained.

Braids and cords

Braids and cords offer yet another, totally different, look. Flat braids are easier to apply before making up your cover, while chunky cords can be hand-sewn round the outside edge of a finished cover. In this case, it is sometimes easier if the cover has its pad added first, as the edge then becomes more prominent and the result is apparent while the cord is being added. Flanged cords and braids – those attached to a flat tape – can be added in the same way as covered piping cord (see pages 32–33).

MATERIALS: *Braided cushion, 46 x 36cm (18 x 14in):* 46cm (½yd) of furnishing fabric, 140cm (55in) wide; 160cm (1¾yd) of 2.5cm (1in) wide decorative braid, same-size cushion pad, matching thread, tape measure, scissors, pins and needles
Corded cushion, 40cm (16in) square: 46cm (½yd) of furnishing fabric, 140cm (55in) wide; 2m (2¼yd) of chunky cord, same-size cushion pad, matching thread, tape measure, scissors, pins and needles

FABRIC: *Braided cushion, front:* Measure the pad width and length and add an extra 3cm (1¼in) seam allowance to both measurements. Cut one rectangle of fabric to this size
Back: Cut another rectangle of fabric the same size as the front but adding an extra 3cm (1¼in) to the width or length for a centre-back opening. Cut the back into two equal pieces
Corded cushion, front: Measure the pad width and length and add 3cm (1¼in) seam allowance to both measurements. Cut one square of fabric to this size
Back: Cut one piece of fabric to the same size as the front but adding an extra 3cm (1¼in) seam allowance to the width or length for the centre-back opening. Cut the back into two equal pieces

BRAIDED CUSHION

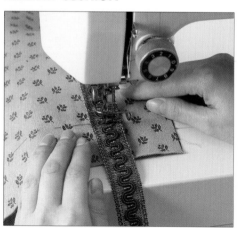

1 Mark a guide-line for the braid on the right side of the front cushion piece, using tacking stitches 4.5cm (1¾in) in from the outer edge (this will ensure it is clearly displayed on the cushion).

Beginning at the centre of the base edge, lay the braid right side up along the first edge, with the outer edge alongside the marked line; pin and tack. Stitch along the outer edge of the braid only, up to the first corner.

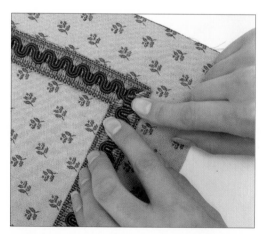

2 At the corner, fold the braid straight back over the stitched section in a neat diagonal, ready to run down along the next side. Press firmly.

3 Lift the braid up and stitch across the corner on its reverse side, along the diagonal pressed line. Fold the braid back along the next edge and stitch only along its outer edge to the next corner, making sure that all stitching is matched up in straight lines. Fasten the thread ends on the wrong side. Repeat in order to stitch each corner in the same way.

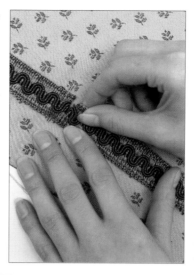

4 Join the trimmed ends of the braid together centrally on the base edge. Complete by stitching along the inner edge of the braid. Add a fastening into the centre-back seam and complete the cushion in the usual way.

CORDED CUSHION

1 Here you are simply hand-sewing a heavyweight cord round the outer edge of a cover. Make up the cover with a centre-back opening in the usual way. Beginning in the centre of the base edge, lay the cord along the seam line. Hand-sew the cord to the seamline. At each corner, tie a knot in the cord before stitching along the next edge.

2 At the centre of the base, carefully snip one stitch of the seam and form a small gap. Carefully unravel the cord ends. Cross over the cord ends and push into the gap. Sew the seam closed again neatly, enclosing the cord-ends.

Fabric tassels

In this style idea, create your own fabric tassels in matching material for an unusual but distinctive look. Add them to a basic cushion made up with a simple slipstitched opening in one edge. In future, you might like to see what effects you can get by using tassel material that contrasts with the cover in some way – plain tassels and a patterned cover, for example.

MATERIALS: *40cm (16in) square cover with 20cm (8in) long tassels:* 1.2m (1⅜yd) of furnishing fabric, 140cm (55in) wide; dressmakers' squared pattern paper, same-size cushion pad, matching thread, small amount of wadding or filling, cotton perle embroidery thread, tape measure, scissors, pins and needles

FABRIC: *Front and back:* Measure the pad widthways and lengthways and add 3cm (1¼in) seam allowance to both measurements. Cut two squares of fabric to this size.
Tassels: Draw up the pattern for the tassel as shown in step 1 and cut out eight times

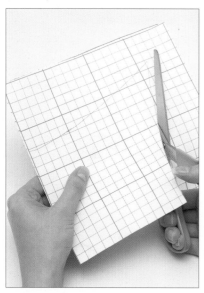

1 Make up the cushion cover in the usual way. Cut a 40cm (16in) square of pattern paper. Fold the paper in half both ways. Draw up the pattern shown here onto the folded paper. Cut out the pattern and unfold the paper. Cut out eight pieces of fabric to this pattern.

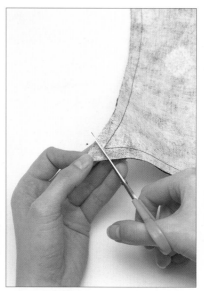

2 For each tassel, place two tassel pieces with right sides together. Pin, tack and stitch them together all round, taking 1cm (⅜in) seam allowance and leaving an opening for turning the pieces the right way round. Trim off the corners and turn the tassel right side out.

3 Thread a needle with a double sewing thread and knot the end. On the wrong side of the tassel, 5cm (2in) from the centre and through all the thicknesses, mark out a square, making a small stitch at each corner before taking the thread to the next corner. Roll up a small ball of wadding or filling and place in the centre of the marked-out square.

4 Pull up the stitches to enclose the wadding and so form the head of the tassel. Round off the head, adjusting as necessary. Secure the head by threading a length of cotton embroidery perle and wind it round, just beneath the wadded head, five or six times. Fasten off and thread the end inside the bound threads.

corner of the cushion cover, stitching through the top of the tassel head.

6 Make three more tassels in the same way and add these to your cover.

Piping

Piping is basically a strip of bias fabric that is folded in half and inserted into a seam. Cord can be added inside the folded fabric, giving a harder edge. Piping cord comes in a variety of thicknesses, and those between 3 and 6 look best on cushions. Select piping to suit the style of your cushions by wrapping the piping fabric round different thicknesses of cord until you get the result you want. Create added interest by ruching up the covering fabric – cut the bias strips in the usual way, but allow two to three times the length of the piping cord. With piped designs, place your opening in the middle of one edge, behind the cord, or across the back of the cushion. Round the corners off gently as for frilled cushions (see pages 26–27), if wished.

MATERIALS: *Piped cushion 38cm (15in) square:* 60cm (³⁄₄yd) of furnishing fabric, 140cm (55in) wide; 1.70m (2yd) of piping cord, same-sized cushion pad, matching thread, tape measure, scissors, needles and pins

FABRIC: *Front and back:* Measure the pad width and length and add 3cm (1¼in) seam allowance to both measurements. Cut two pieces of fabric to this size. For a centre-back opening, add an extra 3cm (1¼in) seam allowance to the width or length of the cushion back and cut the back into two equal pieces.
Piping: Measure the length of one side of the cushion pad and multiply by four, then add an extra 10cm (4in) for joining. For the width, measure round the piping cord and add 3cm (1¼in) seam allowance. Cut sufficient fabric strips across the fabric bias, which, when seamed together, come to the desired length

1 Cut out the bias strips. Pin, tack and stitch the strips together into one long length, taking 5mm (¼in) seams. Fold the bias strip evenly in half round a length of piping cord. Using a piping foot, machine-stitch alongside the cord to hold it in place.

2 On a square cover, position the piping along each side of the front cushion piece in turn, matching the raw edges of piping with the raw edges of the cover, as shown. At each corner, snip into the piping fabric up to the stitching to help form sharp corners.

3 On round covers, snip into the piping fabric at regular intervals, approximately 2.5cm (1in) apart, to help ease the piping round the cover.

4 Pin, tack and stitch the piping in place, ending the stitching 5cm (2in) before the join. Trim the piping so that it overlaps the opposite end by 2.5cm (1in). Unpick 2.5cm (1in) of the stitching from each end of the piping. Trim the cord so that the ends butt together exactly. Turn under the last 1.5cm (⅝in) of piping strip and overlap the opposite end. Pin, tack and finish stitching the piping into position.

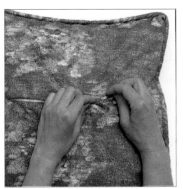

5 Make up the cushion back with a central closure. Place the cushion front and back with their right sides together. Pin, tack and machine-stitch all round the cover, close to the piping, using a piping foot. Trim and turn right side out. Press so that the piping is right at the edge. Insert the pad and slipstitch the opening closed.

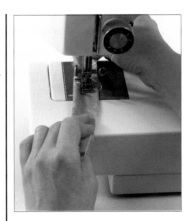

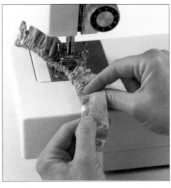

GATHERED PIPING

1 Place the cord inside the bias strip in the same way as for corded piping. Stitch across the end of the folded strip, catching in the end of the cord. Pin, tack and stitch alongside the cord, but not tight up against it, for approximately 20cm (8in).

2 Leaving the needle in the fabric, raise the machine foot. Gently pull the cord through the fabric to gather the covering. Repeat along the whole length of the cord. Trim off the holding stitches and join the ends together in the usual way, making sure that the fabric gathers up over the join. Make up the cushion in the usual way.

Ties and buttons

Ties always make attractive fasteners, while buttons look really neat with envelope-style covers. In our tied example, straight fabric ties are knotted together at one side of the cover. When the pad is added, the inside flap is clearly visible, so using an attractive contrasting fabric will accentuate the detail. This buttoned cover uses a contrasting half lining to make a border and provide buttons and buttonholes with extra support without affecting the sharp base corners. Cover the buttons with the lining fabric.

MATERIALS: *Cushion with ties 36cm (14in) square :* 46cm (½yd) of striped fabric, 114cm (45in) wide; 20cm (8in) of gingham fabric, 90cm (36in) wide, for flap and ties; same-size cushion pad, matching thread, tape measure, scissors, pins and needles
36cm (14in) square envelope cover with buttons: 60cm (¾yd) furnishing fabric, 114cm (45in) wide; 40cm (½yd) of furnishing fabric, 114cm (45in) wide, for lining; same-size cushion pad, matching thread, three 22mm (¾in) diameter self-covering buttons, tape measure, scissors, needles and pins

FABRIC: *Cushion with ties front and back:* Measure the pad width and length and add 3cm (1¼in) to both measurements. Cut out two squares of fabric to this size. *Flap:* Cut a piece of fabric to the same width as the back and 16cm (6¼in) wide.
Ties: For each of the two tie fastenings, cut two strips of fabric 25 x 9cm (10 x 3½in)
Envelope-style cushion, front and back: Measure the pad widthways and add 3cm (1¼in) seam allowance. *Length:* Measure the length of the pad and add 13.5cm (5¼in) for turn-down flap and seam allowance. Cut two pieces of main fabric to this size for front and back
Lining: Cut two pieces of lining fabric to the same width as the cover but only 25cm (10in) long

CUSHION WITH TIES

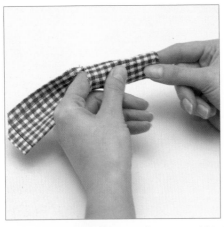

1 Fold one tie piece in half lengthways with right sides facing. Pin, tack and stitch the long side and one short side together,

taking 1cm (⅜in) seam allowance. Trim and turn the tie right side out. Repeat to make up three more ties in the same way.

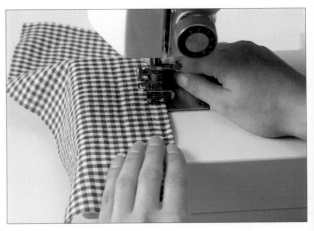

2 Turn under a double 1cm (⅜in) hem along the base edges of the flap. Pin, tack and stitch the hem.

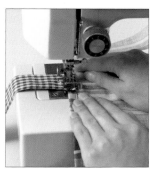

3 Place the raw edges of two ties on the right side edge of the cushion front, 8.5cm (3½in) in from the side edge; pin, tack and stitch. Fold over a double 1cm (⅜in) hem, including the ends of the ties. Pin, tack and stitch the hem.

4 Pin the two remaining ties with their raw edges to the right side edge of the cushion back, matching the front ties. Now place the cover pieces with right sides together, keeping the front hem edge 2cm (¾in) below the outer edge of the back. Place the flap over the top, matching sides and raw edges with the back. Pin, tack and stitch round the cover, avoid catching in the front edge. Trim and turn cover right side out. Insert pad, pushing the flap over it, and knot ties together.

ENVELOPE COVER WITH BUTTONS

1 Place the front and back cushion pieces with right sides together and raw edges matching. Pin, tack and stitch the sides and base edge. Place the lining pieces with their right sides together and raw edges matching; pin, tack and stitch the sides. Turn under a double 1cm (⅜in) hem along the base edge of the lining; pin, tack and stitch hem.

2 Place the lining and fabric covers with right sides together and seams matching. Pin, tack and stitch together round the top edge. Trim and turn the lining up and then press. Push the lining down inside the main cover, leaving a 1cm (⅜in) band of lining showing round the top edge. Pin, tack and stitch all round the top edge, following the first seamline.

3 Fold over the open edge by 12cm (4¾in). Mark positions for three buttonholes, 8.5cm (3½in) in from the side edges and 8.5cm (3½in) apart. Machine-stitch a buttonhole at each marked position through both flap sections. Cover and stitch a button to the cover at each marked position, see pages 18-19 Covering Buttons. Insert the pad and fasten the buttons.

Creative Cushions

Use cushions in a creative way, to echo aspects of your personality and the room's design – you'll be amazed by just how easily your decor can be transformed. Simply choosing an interesting shape or an unusual fabric or trim for a cushion will make all the difference. But why not use your imagination even more? Try making covers from household towels and mats or fashionable scarves. Experiment with cutting and stitching material to form mosaic patterns or twisting it into different shapes with pleats and tucks. Add buttons and trims for colour and interest and cater for children by creating light, bead-filled bags that they will always love to play with. Whatever you choose, your cushions will have that touch of individuality that shop-bought equivalents can't deliver.

Quick covers

Before you embark on a costly search for fabric, try looking round the house for likely materials that could quickly be turned into covers. Tea towels, napkins and place-mats can easily become attractive cushion covers, and those seldom-worn scarves can also be recycled. This approach means that you use the minimum of stitching to create the maximum impact.

MATERIALS: *Laced Tea towel cover for a cushion 35cm (14in) square:* One Tea towel approximately 72 x 51cm (28½ x 20in), 11mm (½in) diameter eyelet kit, cushion pad to fit, 1.2m (1⅓yd) of ribbon 2cm (¾in) wide, in two different colours; tape measure, scissors, pins and needles

Napkin cover for a cushion 38cm (15in) square: Two napkins approximately 48cm (19in) square, matching thread, cushion pad to fit, yarn and bodkin for making pompon, tape measure, scissors, pins and needles

LACED TEA TOWEL COVER

1 Turn in long side edges of tea towel for approximately 8cm (3¼in) and press. Mark and fix pairs of eyelets on either side of the long edges. Place the first pairs 2cm (¾in) and 6cm (2½in) in from long edges, through the towel and the turned-in edge, and just in from the hemmed short edge. Place the next pair 1.5cm (⅝in) either side of the short edge, through the towel only.

2 Place the cushion pad in the centre of the wrong side of the towel, tucking it under the long edges. Take the first length of ribbon and, working from the outer edges, lace up to the centre, tie into a knot to hold the pad in place and then into a bow. Repeat with the second ribbon, from the opposite side into the centre.

MAKING A POMPON

Pompons make an attractive addition to all kinds of cushions. Cut two circles of cardboard 5cm (2in) in diameter, with a central hole 1cm (⅜in) in diameter. Place the rings together and wind wool yarn around them, using a bodkin, until the hole is filled up. Snip through the wool strands, around the outer edge of the card circles. Gently ease the two rings apart and secure the pompon by threading yarn around the centre. Remove the rings.

NAPKIN COVER

1 Pin and tack the two napkins with wrong sides together; topstitch all round, 3.5cm (1½in) from the outer

edge, leaving an opening centrally in one side. Work a second line of stitching beside the first line. Insert pad. Close the opening by completing the two rows of topstitching across it.

2 Make up a 3.5cm (1½in) diameter pompon (see Making a Pompon). Take the long end of yarn from the centre of the pompon, thread this through a needle and push the yarn through the middle of the cushion. Then push it back through again from the other side, pulling the centre of the pad together, and stitch through the base of the pompon to secure.

OTHER QUICK IDEAS

Gathered tea towel cover

Fold a tea towel in half, right sides together, and sew two side seams, leaving the top open. Turn right side out and insert pad. Gather up opening and hold with a rubber band. Tie and knot a piece of velvet ribbon over the rubber band and sew a small bell to each ribbon-end.

Scarf bolster

Lay out a scarf, wrong side up. Place a piece of heavyweight wadding, narrower than the scarf, in the centre and roll the scarf up tightly to form a bolster shape. Hold the gathered scarf ends with rubber bands and then cover these with tied ribbons.

Kids' cushions

Cushions aren't just for decoration and comfort – they can also provide hours of fun for younger members of the family. Fabric cubes filled with ultra-light polystyrene beads provide both building blocks and seats, while ball-shaped cushions are perfect for rolling round the house.

MATERIALS: *Cube-shaped cushion, approximately 30cm (12in) square:* 80cm (⅞yd) of furnishing fabric, 140cm (55in) wide; polystyrene beads for filling, matching thread, tape measure, scissors, pins and needles
Ball-shaped cushion, approximately 58cm (23in) in diameter: Paper for pattern, 60cm (¾yd) of furnishing fabric, 140cm (55in) wide; polystyrene beads for filling, matching thread, tape measure, scissors, pins and needles

FABRIC: *Cube-shaped cushion:* If your fabric has a strong motif, you might like to alter the cushion size so that the motif can be positioned in the centre of each side
Ball-shaped cushion: Make a paper pattern of one section, using the template on pages 90–91. Cut out six times on the straight grain of the fabric, adding 1cm (⅜in) seam allowance all round

CUBE-SHAPED CUSHION

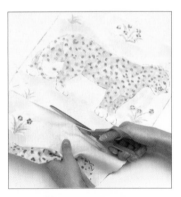

1 Spread out the fabric and carefully mark a 30cm (12in) square (placing any strong motif in the centre). Add 1.5cm (⅝in) seam allowance. Use this square as the template for cutting out five more.

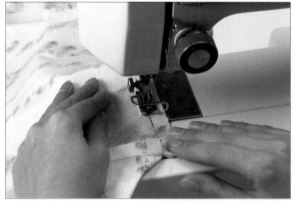

2 Place four squares together in a row. Pin, tack and stitch the four squares into a ring, with right sides together and raw edges matching. Begin and end the stitching 1.5cm (⅝in) from each end of the seams.

3 Place a square at one end of the ring, matching corners to seams. Pin, tack and stitch in place, pivoting the needle at each corner. The side seams will fan out, helping to form sharp corners. Stitch in the last square in the same way, but leaving an opening centrally in one side. Trim seams and turn cube right side out. Fill with polystyrene beads until a nice square shape. Turn in opening edges and hand-sew, making tiny stitches so none of the beads can escape.

BALL-SHAPED CUSHION

1 Place two sections with right sides together and pin, tack and stitch together down one edge. Pin, tack and stitch a third piece to one side – you now have half the ball. Repeat, to make up the second half of the ball.

2 Pin the two halves together into a ring with right sides facing. Pin, tack and stitch together, leaving an opening centrally in one seam.

3 Trim and turn the ball right side out. Carefully fill with polystyrene beads. Turn in opening edges and slipstitch together to close.

FILLING YOUR CUSHION

When filling a shape with polystyrene beads, use a household funnel or make a cone from an old cereal packet and pour your beads through this. This should stop too many from escaping over the floor.

Fun pencil cushion

Try taking interesting and unusual shapes one step further – people of all ages can enjoy cushions with a note of humour. For example, a long pencil shape is quick and easy to make and three pencils in a row makes a practical cushion. Colourful felt is a good material to choose for this style, especially if the cushions are for a child's room.

MATERIALS: One 70cm (28in) square of blue felt, one piece each of orange and green felt 50 x 15cm (20 x 6in), one 15cm (6in) square of navy felt, one piece of beige felt 27 x 16cm (10½ x 6½in), matching threads, 70cm (¾yd) each of blue, orange and green ribbon, 3mm (⅛in) wide, polystyrene beads for filling, tape measure, scissors, pins and needles

FABRIC: *Front:* Draw up patterns for a pencil's body, top, lead and base from those shown on pages 90–91. Cut out three bodies and leads from orange, blue and green felt, three pencil tops from beige felt and three pencil bases from navy. Mark the lines down each body piece. Note: 6mm (¼in) seam allowance and/or overlap has been included in the patterns.

Back: Use the completed cushion front as a template for the back

1 Pin ribbon down each marked line on the pencil bodies. Zigzag stitch over the ribbon. Use blue ribbon on the orange body, orange ribbon on green and green ribbon on blue.

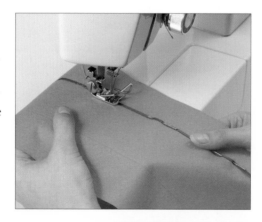

2 For each pencil, put the base piece in position, overlapping the bottom of the pencil body, then satin stitch (a close zigzag stitch) in place and add the pencil top and lead in the same way. Repeat for each pencil.

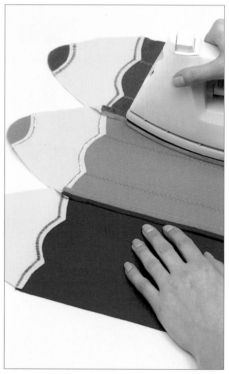

3 Pin, tack and stitch the pencils together in a row. Press the seams firmly open.

4 Use the completed front as a pattern and cut out one complete back section from blue felt. Pin, tack and stitch back to front with right sides facing and leaving the base edge open.

5 Trim and turn right side out. Turn under the base edge 6mm (¼in) and pin. To outline the pencil shapes again, topstitch along the existing seamlines between the pencils. Fill each pencil with beads and sew up the base edge.

Patchwork covers

Patchwork is a perennially popular style – not least because it is simple and ideal for using up all those leftover pieces of fabric. You may think that it has a rather homespun, 'rocking chair' image, but you would be wrong. With a little ingenuity, you can produce unusual effects that are also really stylish.

MATERIALS: *Crazy patchwork cover, 40cm (16in) square:* Assortment of corduroy, velvet and silk in rich colours, plain calico for 'background' fabric, fine cord fabric for the back; matching thread, cotton perle thread in contrasting colour, embroidery needle, same-size cushion pad, tape measure, scissors, pins and needles
Seminole patchwork cover, 40cm (16in) square: Small amount of cotton fabric in four different designs, cotton fabric for cushion back; same-size cushion pad, thread to match main fabric, tape measure, scissors, pins and needles
Cathedral window patchwork cover, 40 x 30cm (16 x 12in): Plain cotton fabric, four different silk fabrics; threads to match each fabric, sequins for decoration, cushion pad to fit, tape measure, scissors, pins and needles

FABRIC: *Crazy patchwork cover, front:* Cut one 43cm (17in) square of background fabric
Back: Cut two pieces fine cord fabric 43 x 23cm (17 x 9in)
Patches: Randomly cut cord, velvet and silk patches in various shapes and sizes
Seminole patchwork cover, front: Consists of 5cm (2in) patchwork squares made up from fabric strips
Back: Cut two pieces, each 43 x 23cm (17 x 9in)
Cathedral window patchwork cover, front: Made up of twelve plain cotton fabric squares, each measuring 21cm (8½in) square. The inset silk squares are 6.5cm (2½in) square

CRAZY PATCHWORK

1 Allow a 1.5cm (⅝in) seam all around background square. Lay patches over the background, and rearrange to your satisfaction. Pin in position.

2 On the overlapping edges of the patches, turn under 6mm (¼in) and tack in place. Slipstitch folded edges in place.

3 Using cotton perle thread and feather stitch, work round the edges of your patches. Make up the cushion back with a central opening (see pages 20–21) and complete the cushion in the usual way.

SEMINOLE PATCHWORK

  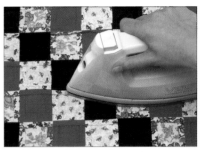

1 Cut 43 x 7cm (17 x 2¾in) strips from each front fabric. With 1cm (⅜in) seam allowances, stitch the strips together then cut strips across the seams 7cm (2¾in) wide.

2 Pin, tack and stitch the strips back together again in a staggered formation, moving the strips down one square as you stitch on each strip.

3 Press the completed front on the reverse side. Make up the back with a central opening (see pages 20–21) and complete the cushion in the usual way.

CATHEDRAL WINDOW PATCHWORK

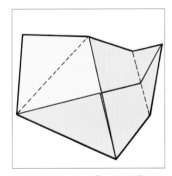

1 For each square, press in 6mm (¼in) on all edges. Fold in half both ways to find the centre. Lay the square wrong side up, fold in each corner to the centre and press. The square should measure 14cm (5½in). Fold in each corner to the centre again; press and pin. The square now measures 10cm (4in). Stab-stitch the four centre points to hold.

2 Make up the cushion front by stitching the squares together into a rectangle. Place the first two squares with folded sides together and oversew the edges. Open out flat and press.

3 Cut 6.5cm (2½in) squares from the different silk fabrics. Pin a square of silk diagonally over each oversewn join. On each edge of the silk square, from the centre, roll back the folds of the backing fabric over the raw edge of the silk, tapering off to a point at each corner. Work a double backstitch at each end, then hand-sew along the rolled back edge, through all the layers. Repeat until the squares form one rectangle. Hand-sew sequins at each intersection. Make up the back with a central opening and complete the cover by hand-sewing back and front together.

Mitres and knots

With just a touch of clever stitching, you can create some really smart cushion covers. Mitred covers depend on careful cutting and pattern-matching for their geometric effect. The triangles of fabric are seamed together to meet at the centre, forming an effective frame — especially successful if you are using fabric with a strong horizontal or vertical pattern. Knotted corners are another attractive feature — basically extended corners which, when tied in a knot, gather the corner to produce a soft, pleasing outline.

MATERIALS: *40cm (16in) square mitred cushion:* Paper for pattern, 80cm (⅞yd) of furnishing fabric, 140cm (55in) wide; cushion pad to fit, matching thread, large bead and complementary yarn, tape measure, scissors, pins and needles
40cm (16in) square cushion with knotted corners: Paper for pattern, 1.5m (1¾yd) of furnishing fabric, 140cm (55in) wide; cushion pad to fit, matching thread, tape measure, scissors, pins and needles

FABRIC: *Square mitred cushion, front:* Draw up a pattern as shown in step 1 and use this to cut the four front triangles
Back: Cut one piece to the size of the cushion pad, adding 3cm (1¼in) seam allowance. For a centre-back opening, add a further 3cm (1¼in) to the width or length and cut in two
Cushions with knotted corners front and back: Draw up the pattern for one half of the cushion, using the template on pages 90–91. Use the pattern to cut out the cushion front, placing the pattern on the fabric fold and add 1.5cm (⅝in) seam allowance to remaining edges. Cut out the back in the same way, but place the pattern 1.5cm (⅝in) from the fabric fold. Cut the back in half down the folded edge

MITRED CUSHION

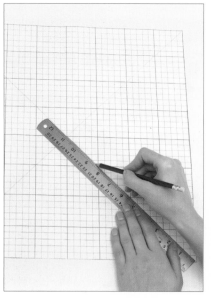

1 Measure the cushion pad and draw a square to this size on a sheet of paper. Carefully rule two diagonal lines from the corners, crossing in the centre. Cut out each triangular piece.

2 Lay the triangles on your fabric so that you get the same part of the fabric's pattern on each one. On striped fabric, the triangular pieces can be placed facing either up or down the fabric, but on a one-way design, position each triangle facing in the same direction. Carefully cut out each piece, adding 1.5cm (⅝in) seam allowance all round.

3 Pin two triangles together, right sides facing and matching the pattern exactly. Tack and stitch down one shorter edge. Repeat with the two remaining triangles.

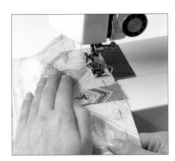

4 Place the two opened-out sets of triangles together, with right sides facing. Pin, tack and stitch together to form the front. Be careful to match the pattern across the seam.

5 Stitch two back pieces together, adding a central fastening if desired (see pages 20–21). Place cushion front and back pieces with right sides facing; pin, tack and stitch together all round. Trim and turn right side out. Hand-sew the bead to the centre front with the yarn. Insert cushion pad and close opening.

CUSHION WITH KNOTTED CORNERS

1 Place back pieces with right sides facing. Pin, tack and stitch together, adding a central opening (see pages 20–21). Place back and front cover pieces with right sides together and matching outer edges. Pin, tack and stitch together all round, taking 1.5cm (⅝in) seam allowance.

2 Trim and turn right side out. Press with seams right to the edge. Insert cushion pad.

3 Knot each extended corner and arrange the ends decoratively.

Pleats and tucks

Classic pleats and tucks provide an understated texture for all kinds of silk cushions. The pleats are stitched in straight lines; in the example shown here, different sized pleats have been used to add interest to a plain silk cover. On the other cushion, 1cm (⅜in) tucks are stitched into a four-sectioned cover, creating a rippling patchwork effect. The squares are seamed together with the tucks lying in different directions.

MATERIALS: *35cm (14in) square pleated cushion:* Tissue paper for pattern, 56cm (⅝yd) of silk 140cm (55in) wide; cushion pad to fit, matching thread, tape measure, scissors, pins and needles
36cm (14in) square tucked cushion: 80cm (⅞yd) of silk 140cm (55in) wide, cushion pad to fit, matching thread, one 29mm (1¼in) diameter self-covering button, tape measure, scissors, pins and needles

FABRIC: *Pleated cushion, front:* Cut a piece of fabric 78 x 38cm (30¾in x 15in).
Back: Measure the cushion pad width and length, adding 3cm (1¼in) seam allowance. Cut one piece of fabric to these measurements, adding an extra 3cm (1¼in) allowance to the width or length for a centre-back fastening
Tucked cushion, front: The front is divided into four equal sections. Cut four pieces of silk, each 53 x 20cm (21 x 8in)
Back: Measure the cushion pad widthways and lengthways and add 3cm (1¼in) seam allowance. Cut one piece of fabric to this size

PLEATED CUSHION

1 Cut a sheet of tissue paper 75 x 38cm (30 x 15in). Draw your pleat arrangement onto the paper. Lay out the front cushion strip, right side up. Pin the tissue paper pattern onto the fabric, with the ends 1.5cm (⅝in) in from the short edges. Tack through the paper and fabric along each line. Then carefully pull away the paper, leaving the tacking stitches in place.

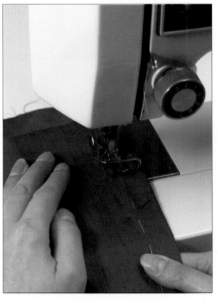

2 Form each pleat by folding the fabric with wrong sides together, matching two lines of tacking stitches together. Pin, tack and stitch. Form each pleat in the same way.

3 Press each pleat along the fold and then press all the pleats so that they lie in the same direction. Tack all round the outer edge, over the seamlines, catching down the pleats.

4 Place back and front pieces with right sides facing and outer edges matching. Pin, tack and stitch round outer edge, leaving a central opening in the base. Trim and turn cushion right side out. Insert cushion pad; turn in opening edges and slipstitch to close.

TUCKED CUSHION

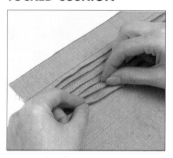

1 Beginning 2cm (¾in) from one short end, fold, pin and stitch 1cm (⅜in) wide tucks right across the first of your four front sections, making it a square. Press all the tucks facing in one direction. Stitch down either side to hold the tucks. Mark a line down the centre and stitch against the direction of the tucks.

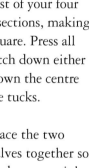

2 Make up each square in the same way. Take the first two squares and pin together with the tucks at right angles to each other; pin, tack and stitch together. Stitch the second pair of squares together in the same way.

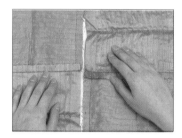

3 Place the two halves together so the tucks are at right angles to each other. Pin, tack and stitch together to complete the cushion front.

4 Place front and back together with right sides facing. Pin, tack and stitch all round, leaving a base edge opening. Trim and turn right side out. Cover the button with fabric to match the cover (see Covering Buttons, pages 18–19) and sew to the centre of the cover. Insert cushion pad and slipstitch opening to close.

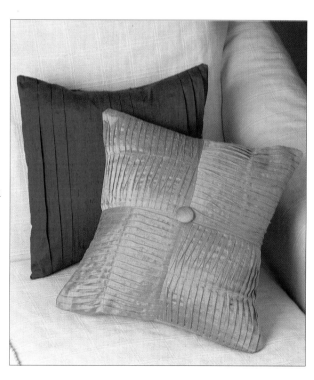

A touch of glamour

Sumptuous cushion covers are an inexpensive way to add a touch of sophisticated glamour to your home. So, when choosing fabric for this kind of cover, walk past the furnishing and dressmaking fabrics and head for beautiful velvets and silks in rich colours – not only will they look good, but they are wonderful to the touch.

MATERIALS: *Square cushion 30cm (12in) with 10cm (4in) wide border:* Paper for pattern, 40cm (16in) square devoré velvet; 80cm (⅞yd) of silk 115cm (45in) wide; 120cm (1⅓yd) of gold-coloured tubing, gold thread, same-size cushion pad, thread to match fabric, tape measure, scissors, pins and needles

FABRIC: *Front:* Cut two centre squares, one from velvet and one from silk, adding 1.5cm (⅝in) all round for seam allowances
Back: Cut as front, from silk only, adding 3cm (1¼in) for the back opening; cut in half.
Border: Fold border fabric in half, placing long outer edge of paper pattern on the folded edge. Add 1.5cm (⅝in) seam allowance on all remaining sides and cut four border sections from silk

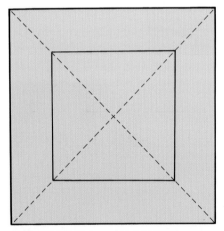

1 Make a pattern by measuring the pad width and length and draw on paper a square to this size. Draw a second square 10cm (4in) outside the first square – this will be the border outer edge. Mark lines diagonally across the square to ensure accurate seams at each corner. Cut out the border and centre square patterns and use to cut four border pieces and three centre squares.

2 Open out each border section and, with right sides facing, tack and sew the corner edges together to form a frame, stitching 1.5cm (⅝in) from inner edge. Trim and press seams open. Refold into border and press. Tack inner edges of border together.

3 Lay the velvet, right side up, over the silk central square. Pin and tack together diagonally across the square, in both directions, and 1.5cm (⅝in) in from the outer edge. This will hold the two layers in position.

4 Place inner edge of border to right side of centre square, matching the edges. Pin, tack and stitch all round, following marked seamline. Pin, tack and stitch back sections together, adding a central fastening. Place back over front with right sides together and with the border carefully folded inside; pin, tack and stitch together all round the outer edge. Trim and turn cover right side out through the central opening.

5 Insert cushion pad and close fastening. Hand-sew gold-coloured tubing round the seamline between central pad and border, by catching over the tubing at 6.5cm (2½in) intervals along each side and at each corner. Be careful not to catch in the cushion pad.

Exotic cushions

Your imagination can run wild with these deliciously indulgent cushions. Let the fabrics speak for themselves, or add extravagant decoration – in these examples, beaded fringing complements the brocade, while ruched piping gives the fur cushion a nicely rounded border that is both simple and stylish.

MATERIALS: *Brocade and beaded cushion, 40 x 30cm (16 x 12in):* 46cm (½yd) of brocade 115cm (45in) wide; 1.5m (1⅔yd) of 8cm (3in) wide 'fringed' beaded trim, 1.5m (1⅔yd) of ribbon 1.5cm (⅝in) wide, 1.8m (2yd) of silver bead trim, matching thread, cushion pad to fit, tape measure, scissors, pins and needles
Fun-fur cushion, 36cm (14in): 46cm (½yd) fun-fur fabric 90cm (36in) wide; 50cm (⅝yd) striped silk fabric 115cm (45in) wide, tieback piping or rolled wadding, matching threads, same-size cushion pad, tape measure, scissors, pins and needles

FABRIC: *Brocade cushion front and back:* Measure the pad length and width and add 3cm (1¼in) seam allowance to both measurements. Cut out two pieces of fabric to these measurements
Fun-fur cushion, front: Measure the pad both ways and cut a piece of fur fabric to this size, add 1.5cm (⅝in) all round for seam allowance
Back: Cut one piece of fur fabric the same size as the front, adding an extra 3cm (1¼in) to the width for the central seam allowance; cut in half
Piping: Cut silk strips 10cm (4in) wide to fit round the piping. Measure around the pad and make piping twice this length

BROCADE AND BEADS

1 Tack a line of stitches around the cushion front as a guide for positioning the ribbon. Place the ribbon to the inside of the tacked outline and pin and tack in position, mitring the corners. Machine-stitch or hand-sew the ribbon in place.

2 Pin and tack the bead fringe to the right side of the cushion front, placing the tape along the tacked line. Join tape ends together carefully, so the lengths of beads are evenly spaced over the join. For fullness at each corner, gather in an extra 7.5cm (3in) of tape and tack in place. Stitch the bead trim to cushion front.

3 Place cushion back to front with right sides together. Pin, tack and stitch all round, leaving a central base edge opening. Trim and turn right side out. Sew silver bead trim round the outer edge of the cushion, forming small loops over each corner. Insert pad. Turn under edges of opening and slipstitch to close.

FUN-FUR

1 Pin, tack and stitch the silk covering strips together to obtain the desired length. Fold it round the piping cord and pin, tack and stitch down the length for about 20cm (8in) – do not stitch close to the cord.

2 After 20cm (8in), leave the needle in the fabric and gently ease the cord through the fabric, creating a gathered effect. Continue in this way until you have stitched down the complete length.

3 Working from the wrong side, tack a guideline 1.5cm (⅝in) from the outer edge of the cushion front. Pin ruched piping round the cushion front, with raw edges matching. Join the ends together to fit the base edge.

4 Tack and stitch the piping in place. Make up the back with a central opening, in the usual way (see pages 20–21), and complete the cover.

Scented cushions

Lightly scented cushions bring the sweet smell of summer into the house all year round. Each cushion contains a mixture of scented petals and herbs that will add fragrance to a room as well as promoting peaceful sleep.

MATERIALS: *Lace mat cushion, approximately 25 x 22cm (10 x 8¾in):* Paper for pattern, 46cm (½yd) of cotton fabric 90cm (36in) wide, lace mat or doily, 50cm (⅝yd) of lace edging 25mm (1in) wide, 1.6m (1¾yd) of ribbon 6mm (¼in) wide, matching thread, medium-weight wadding for filling, handful of pot pourri, scrap of pink net, tape measure, scissors, pins and needles
Scented rose cushion, 30cm (12in) square: 46cm (½yd) of rose print fabric 90cm (36in) wide; 30 x 15cm (12 x 6in) piece of white net, 1m (1⅛yd) of ribbon 6mm (¼in) wide, 1.40m (1½yd) of white scalloped trimming, four ribbon roses, cushion pad to fit, matching thread, small amount of pot pourri, tape measure, scissors, pins and needles

FABRIC: *Lace mat cushion, front and back:* Draw up an oval paper pattern to chosen size and cut out two pieces of fabric, adding 1.5cm (⅝in) seam allowance all round for front and back cushion pieces
Rose cushion, front and back: Measure the cushion pad lengthways and widthways and add 3cm (1¼in) seam allowance. Cut two pieces of fabric to these measurements for front and back cushion pieces

LACE MAT CUSHION

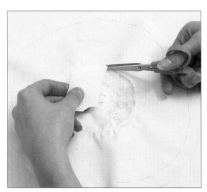

1 Pin and tack the lace mat centrally to the front cover piece. Machine-stitch all round, following the outline of the mat and then zigzag stitch over the same line. Trim away fabric from behind the lacy sections. Zigzag stitch round the cut edges again, working from the wrong side.

2 Tack round the front cushion piece, 1.5cm (⅝in) from the outer edge, to mark the seamline. Pin and tack the lace edging round the cushion front, following the tacked outline.

3 For the frill, cut fabric strips 6.5cm (2½in) wide and, twice the length of the circumference. Stitch together into a ring with French seams. Press a 3mm (⅛in) hem to the right side. Pin the ribbon against the outside edge, covering the raw edges of fabric. Stitch down both sides of the ribbon.

4 Gather up the frill with large machine stitches round the raw edges of the frill. Pull up to fit the outer edge of the oval and pin over the lace edging. Place the back and front together, with lace and frill in between; pin, tack and stitch, leaving a base edge opening; turn right side out.

5 Using t... cut two p... wadding. Cut a... square of pink n... net centrally on w...ing and loosely tack round the outer edges. Add a sprinkling of pot pourri between the two layers of wadding. Slide the wadding into the cushion. Turn in opening edges and close.

SCENTED ROSE CUSHION

1 Lay the cushion's front piece right side up. Cut two 15cm (6in) squares of net. Place one on top of the other and pin and tack the net onto the centre of the cushion front. Cut ribbon into four equal lengths. Pin, tack and stitch two ribbons on either side of the net square, just overlapping the raw edges.

2 Add the two remaining ribbons on the two remaining sides of the net square. Before stitching down the last ribbon, push some pot pourri under the net square. Trim the ribbon ends into Vs.

3 Pin and tack the white scallop trimming round the outer edge of the front piece. Place the front and back pieces with right sides together over the trimming; pin, tack and stitch, leaving an opening in one side. Trim any fraying edges with pinking shears and turn right side out.

4 Hand-sew a ribbon rose onto each corner of the net square. Insert the pad. Turn in the edges of the opening and slipstitch to close.

Floor and Seating Cushions

As well as scattering attractive cushions around your chairs and sofas, you may want to use them to create comfortable and attractive seating – both indoors and outdoors. Large floor cushions provide highly adaptable additions to any room, kitchen chairs and wooden benches usually need comfortable padding, and lazing around outside in a deckchair is much more enjoyable with some specially designed cushioned support.

Floor cushion

Floor cushions are always handy as informal extra seating. These enormous wedge-shaped cushions are filled with soft polystyrene beads and tied together to create a series of comfortable shapes. The one shown here can also be turned quickly into an overnight bed, two pairs of wedges tied together are just the answer when you're short on space. Mix and match a variety of different fabrics for a cheerful effect.

MATERIALS: 2.5m (2¾yd) of cotton furnishing fabric, 150cm (60in) wide; 3.90m (4⅜yd) of tape 1cm (⅜in) wide for ties, polystyrene beads for filling, matching threads, tape measure, scissors, pins and needles

FABRIC (for each cushion):
Top: Cut one piece 90cm (36in) square
Bottom: Cut one piece 90 x 80cm (36 x 31½in)
Back: Cut one piece 90 x 40cm (36 x 16in)
Sides: Cut two triangles with 80cm (31½in) base edges and a 40cm (16in) back edge. The diagonal edge should be 90cm (36in) long

1 Make up 13 ties in the same way. Cut a 30cm (12in) length of tape. Fold in half to form a 15cm (6in) length. Topstitch all round.

2 Pin the ties in place on each piece, matching raw ends to fabric edges. As shown, position three ties along one edge of the top piece, 1.5cm (⅜in) in from each outer edge, and one in the centre. Position three ties on each long edge of the back piece and a tie centrally in the base and diagonal edges of each side piece.

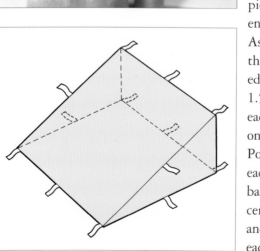

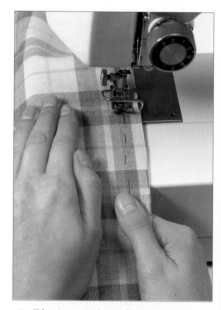

3 Placing right sides together; pin, tack and stitch the top to the bottom and to the back, beginning and ending 1.5cm (⅜in) from each edge and leaving a small opening in the back/bottom seam. Catch in the tie ends.

4 Pin, tack and stitch the sides into each end; the seams will split open at the ends to form neat corners. Trim and turn right side out.

5 Fill generously with beads and close opening with very small hand stitches or by machine-stitching across the opening.

Squab seat

Most kitchen chairs benefit from the addition of a padded 'squab' seat, and removable cushions are the obvious choice as these coverings need to be easy to launder. The decorative element is supplied by the way in which the cushion is anchored to the chair – try matching or contrasting ties made from left-over fabric, elaborate ribbon ties that criss-cross down the chair leg, or large fabric bows. For a more restrained look, fix decorative press studs or loops and toggle fastenings. A deeper pad can be made by adding a narrow 4cm (1½in) gusset between the two cushion pieces.

MATERIALS: Paper for template, 46cm (½yd) furnishing fabric, 90cm (36in) wide; 1.40m (1½yd) of piping cord, 30cm (12in) contrast fabric 90cm (36in) wide for covering piping and toggle strips, two toggle buttons, 6mm (¼in) elastic, matching thread, wadding for filling, tape measure, scissors, pins and needles

FABRIC: *Top and bottom:* Use a paper pattern to cut two pieces from your fabric, adding 1.5cm (⅝in) seam allowance all round
Ties: For each toggle-loop, cut a strip of fabric 14 x 2cm (5½ x ¾in). For each plain loop, cut a strip of fabric 20 x 2cm (8 x ¾in)
Piping: Measure round the edge of the pattern and make up covered piping to this length plus 4cm (1½in) (for joining see page 32-33)

1 Lay a sheet of paper over the chair seat. Holding the paper firmly in position, mark round the outer edge of the seat, curving in around the chair-back at the back corners. Carefully cut round the pattern outline, snipping-in around the back struts to ensure a good fit. Mark back strut position on the pattern for the ties.

2 Using the pattern, cut two fabric pieces and mark the tie positions with pins. Add a line of stitching to reinforce back corners. With cover right side up, pin and tack the piping round one cover piece, matching the raw edges. Snip into the curves. Join the covered piping cord in the centre of the back edge.

3 Make up two toggle-loops by folding a fabric strip in half lengthways, with right sides facing; pin and stitch down the length, taking 6mm (¼in) seam allowance. Turn right side out. Cut an 11cm (4½in) length of elastic and slide inside the tube; pin at both ends to hold.

4 Make up two plain loops in the same way as the toggle loops, but with 14cm (5½in) lengths of elastic. Fold each loop in half and place over the piping at the marked positions at back of cushion. Pin and tack to hold.

5 Place the second cushion piece over the first one with right sides facing and outer edges matching. Pin, tack and stitch together all round, leaving an opening centrally in the back edge between the tie positions. Trim and turn right side out. Use the paper pattern to cut out the wadding. Insert wadding, turn in opening edges and slipstitch together to close. Hand-sew a toggle centrally on the inside of each toggle loop.

Bench seat

Wooden bench seats are ideal for use in the garden during the summer, and can then be brought inside for the winter months. Choose stylish, checked fabric and for additional comfort, reinforce the outer edges with a soft, rolled wadding edge, hand-stitched into position. A boxed cushion to fit any size seat can be made by the same method.

MATERIALS: (Materials will vary according to the size of the seat) Foam pad, 7.5cm (3in) thick, the same size as the seat, 1m (1¼yd) furnishing fabric 150cm (60in) wide, 2.2m (2½yd) wadding, 90cm (36in) wide, 1.2m (1¾yd) lining fabric 137cm (54in) wide, Velcro fastening tape 15cm (6in) shorter than length of pad, matching thread and buttonhole thread, tape measure, scissors, pins and needles

FABRIC: Cut all the pieces from fabric, wadding and lining.
Top and bottom: Measure the foam pad and cut two pieces to this size, adding 1.5cm (⅝in) seam allowance, plus 2cm (¾in) for padded edge, all round
Gusset: For the back gusset, cut two pieces 15cm (6in) shorter than pad length and half the depth. Add seam allowance all round, plus 2cm (¾in) padded allowance to long outer edges. For the other gusset piece which forms the front and sides, cut one piece, the length of the circumference minus length of back gusset, adding 1.5cm (⅝in) seam allowance all round and 2cm (¾in) padded edge allowance. The opening is placed centrally across the gusset back

1 Layer each fabric piece by placing wadding and lining to the wrong side of the fabric. Pin and tack all the pieces together.

2 Make up the gusset as shown. To make the opening, separate Velcro and position each half over the central seam allowance. Pin, tack and stitch in place. Press Velcro together and join the front and sides gusset piece to each end of the back gusset, making a ring.

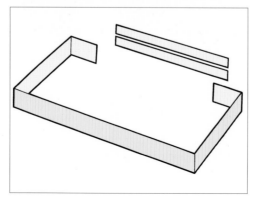

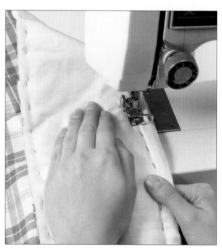

3 Pin, tack and stitch gusset to cushion top and bottom, placing the back opening centrally across the back edge, and with right sides facing and outer edges matching. Snip into the gusset at each corner to help form sharp corners. Turn cushion right side out.

4 Using buttonhole thread, stab-stitch through the layers 2cm (¾in) in from the seamline. This will create a padded, rolled edge. Continue stitching all round the top and bottom edge.

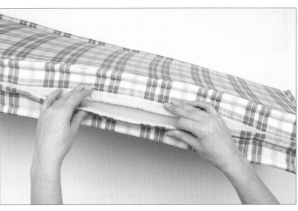

5 Insert the foam pad, fitting it neatly into the corners, and close back opening.

Deckchair cushions

Cushions for the garden should be brightly coloured, simple to wash and quick and easy to store away. Size your cushions so they will lie right across the width of your deckchair, providing maximum comfort. Add corner eyelets so that they can be strung together with large split curtain rings, cords or tapes – these will also anchor them round the top struts of the chair, fixing a pillow cushion firmly in place. Fill each cushion with a washable polyester filling, or make up the cushions so the covers can easily be removed for cleaning.

MATERIALS: *For each cushion:* 46cm (½yd) of cotton furnishing fabric 90cm (36in) wide; washable filling, 11mm (⅜in) diameter eyelet kit, 2.5cm (1in) split curtain rings, matching thread, tape measure, scissors, pins and needles, cord or tape

FABRIC: *Front:* For each cushion, cut one piece 40cm (16in) wide 28cm (11in) deep adding 1.5cm (⅝in) seam allowance all round.
Back: For each back, cut two pieces 28 x 23cm (11 x 9in) adding 1.5cm (⅝in) seam allowance all round

1 Place back pieces with right sides facing. Pin and stitch 9cm (3½in) seams from each side of the shorter length to make the central opening. Press seam and opening flat.

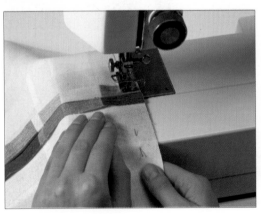

2 Place cushion back to cushion front with right sides facing. Pin, tack and stitch together all round. Trim and turn cover right side out, through back opening. Press with seam out to the edge.

3 Topstitch all round the outer edge of the cover. To accommodate the eyelets create a border all round the cover. Pin and stitch a seamline 2.5cm (1in) from the outer edges.

4 Following the manufacturer's instructions, mark and fix an eyelet into each corner of the cover. Insert filling and slipstitch closed.

5 To join the cushions together, fix a split ring into each eyelet and then link together – or use lengths of cord or tape. Fix the upper cushion round the top struts of the deckchair.

Hand-stitched Cushions

Really lovely cushions can be conjured up from pieces of clever stitch-work such as quilting, appliqué, crewelwork, embroidery or needlepoint – a practical and attractive way of showing off your skills. Most forms of needlecraft can be translated into a cushion cover – just vary the cushion size to suit the various methods.

This chapter contains

Quilted cushions

Several types of quilting can be used very successfully for cushion covers. Two approaches are shown here – trapunto and Italian quilting. With trapunto quilting, a motif is outlined with handstitching and then stuffed from behind to produce raised areas. Italian quilting has evenly worked channels of stitching through which cords are pulled to form round furrows. When using sheer fabrics, the hues of the cord show through on the right side, adding strips of colour.

MATERIALS: *Trapunto cushion, 30cm (12in) square:* 46cm (½yd) of furnishing fabric 137cm (54in) wide (with a prominent motif), 33cm (13in) square muslin, small amount of filling, cotton perle thread in a contrasting colour, matching thread, same-size cushion pad, tape measure, scissors, pins and needles
Italian-quilted cushion, 30cm (12in) square:
40cm (16in) square of shiny, sheer fabric, 46cm (½yd) plain cotton poplin 90cm (36in) wide, green rug wool, matching thread, same-size cushion pad, tape measure, scissors, pins and needles

FABRIC: *Trapunto quilting, front:* Cut one 33cm (13in) square from fabric. Make sure that the main motif is centred on the fabric piece
Back: Cut two pieces, each 33 x 18cm (13 x 7in)
Italian quilted cushion, front: Cut two 36cm (14in) squares, one from sheer fabric and one from poplin
Back: Cut two pieces of poplin, 33 x 18cm (13 x 7in)

TRAPUNTO QUILTING

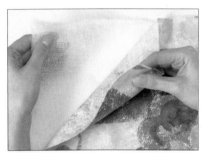

1 Pin and tack the muslin to the wrong side of the fabric, matching outer edges.

2 Using cotton perle and working from the right side, hand-stitch round the main areas of the motif with small running stitches.

3 On the wrong side, gently ease the threads of the muslin apart behind each stitched area and push in small amounts of filling until you create a firm, rounded effect. Push back the threads and hold with a few handstitches, if necessary, to keep the filling firmly in place. Make up a cushion back in the usual way and complete the cushion.

ITALIAN QUILTING

1 Tack the sheer fabric, right side up, onto the cotton poplin, working across the fabric at regular intervals to stop the sheer fabric sliding. On paper, roughly work out a pattern for the channels – each channel will be 6.5mm (¼in) wide.

2 Using the sewing machine foot as a guide, stitch across the fabric to form a series of channels. Always work in the same direction.

3 Thread the rug wool onto a bodkin and thread through each channel, leaving at least 8cm (3in) hanging free at each end, until all the channels have been filled.

4 To secure the ends of the channels, stitch a line round the fabric, 1.25cm (½in) in from the edge. Trim the overhanging wool to the edge of the fabric. Make up the cushion back with a central opening and complete the cushion in the usual way.

Appliqué ideas

Appliqué – the art of applying one fabric to another – has been used to embellish clothes and furnishings in all kinds of imaginative ways for centuries. Two popular forms are felt appliqué, which uses simple, almost childlike cut-outs to great effect, and appliqué perse, where motifs from one fabric are cut out and applied to another, in effect creating a third type of fabric.

MATERIALS: *Two felt appliqué cushions, 35cm (14in) and 40cm (16in) square:* Paper for pattern, small cushion: 46cm (½yd) of ribbed cotton fabric 90cm (36in) wide, 30cm (12in) square of blue felt, larger cushion: 50cm (⅝yd) of ribbed cotton fabric, 90cm wide, 36cm (14in) square of blue felt, fusible webbing, thread to match felt, square cushion pads, button (optional), tape measure, scissors, pins and needles

Perse appliqué 30cm (12in) square: 46cm (½yd) striped fabric 90cm (36in) wide, 33cm (13in) square net fabric, fabric with fish motifs, fusible webbing, thread to match background, small shells and starfish that can be sewn on, small beads, small white plastic curtain rings, 1.6m (1¾yd) white piping cord, same-size cushion pad, tape measure, scissors, pins and needles

FABRIC: *Felt appliqué, front:* Measure the pad both ways and cut one piece of ribbed cotton to this size, adding 1.5cm (⅝in) seam allowance all round
Back: Cut back the same size as the front, adding an extra 1.5cm (⅝in) seam allowance to one edge. Cut into two equal pieces
Felt decoration: Cut one square of felt 3.5cm (1½in) smaller than cushion front
Appliqué perse front: From striped fabric and from net, cut one 33cm (13in) square
Back: Cut two pieces of striped fabric, 33 x 18cm (13 x 7in)

FELT APPLIQUÉ

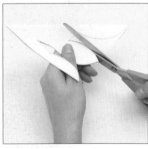

1 Cut a square of paper 3.5cm (1½in) smaller than the chosen cushion size. Fold in half both ways, and then diagonally. Draw your design on the triangle, remembering that the folds will produce a double-size pattern. Cut out with pointed scissors or craft knife.

2 Iron fusible webbing onto one side of the felt. Unfold your paper pattern and use to mark the design onto the paper side of the webbing. Cut out.

3 Peel off the protective paper, centre the felt design on the cushion front and fuse in position.

4 Stitch round the outline of the design. Pull all the sewing threads to the wrong side and fasten off. Make up a cushion back and complete cushion in the usual way.

APPLIQUÉ PERSE

1 Roughly cut out four fish from fabric. Iron fusible webbing to the wrong side. Carefully cut out each fish round the outline.

2 Mark the centre of cushion front. Position the fish so all face into the centre. Peel off the protective backing and fuse fish in place with an iron. Pin and tack the net square over the cushion front.

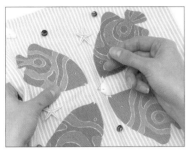

3 Make up cushion back and place to cushion front with right sides together. Pin and stitch all round. Trim and turn right side out. Carefully hand-sew beads, shells and starfish onto the cover, catching down the netting at various points.

4 Hand-sew a white plastic curtain ring at each corner and in the centre of each side. Thread heavy white piping cord through all the rings and knot together at one corner.

Crewelwork cover

Crewelwork is freehand embroidery worked on fabric with embroidery wools. Motifs are often taken from nature – flowers, fruits and birds – each one worked in even rows of filling stitch such as chain stitch or individual stitches, seed stitch, for example. By using fine stranded wool the effects are intricate and delicate and the resulting style is a true-to-life picture.

MATERIALS: Tracing paper and pencil, two pieces of linen cloth 57cm (22½in) square, 30cm (12in) cushion pad, dressmakers' pencil, DMC Medici wool, one skein each of the colours shown on the chart (see pages 74–75), small crewel needle, sewing needle and tacking thread, tape measure, scissors and pins

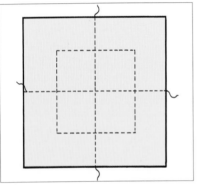

1 To prepare the fabric, measure and mark the centre of one piece of linen. Tack a line vertically and horizontally across the fabric to find the centre. Measure and mark a central square 30cm (12in). Tack all round the square.

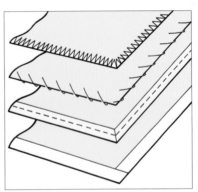

2 To prevent fraying, use any of the following: zigzag stitch all round the edge of the linen by machine, oversew by hand, turn under the edge and stitch, or fold masking tape over the edges. There should be a border of around 7.5cm (3in) around the design area.

3 Trace off the same-size design from pages 74–75 onto tracing paper. To transfer the design onto the fabric, tape the traced design onto a light window and tape the fabric centrally over the top. Use the dressmakers' pencil to trace the design onto the fabric. Take down the design and go over any faint sections.

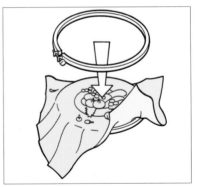

4 You will find it much easier to embroider if you fit your fabric into a special embroidery hoop. Separate the two rings by loosening the screw on the larger ring and placing the fabric centrally over the smaller one. Gently press the larger hoop over the top. Now tighten the screw until the fabric is taut inside the loop.

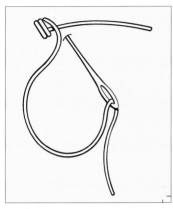

5 Following the chart and key on pages 74–75, work mostly with a double thickness of wool, although some of the fine lines should be worked with a single strand. For details of the stitches used, see Embroidery Stitches, pages 88–89. To start stitching, use a 40cm (16in) length of wool and bring it up through the fabric at the desired position. Holding the end of the wool at the back, work a few stitches over the end. For subsequent lengths, run the needle under a few stitches on the wrong side. To end a length, run the needle under a few stitches on the wrong side and trim off end.

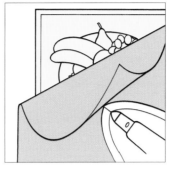

6 When the embroidery is complete, place the work face down on a soft cloth and press the back lightly with a steam iron. Leave to go cold before moving it.

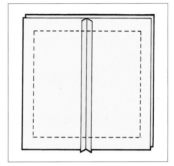

7 Make up into a cushion using the preferred fastening method (see pages 20–21). With right sides facing; pin, tack and stitch the back and front covers together to complete.

TIME-SAVING TIP
To save time, thread several needles with all the colours needed for the area on which you are working and simply switch needles for each colour.

In this example an overlapping vent fastening was used. A border was created by handstitching a decorative inner seamline 5cm (2in) in from the outer edge following the dimensions of the cushion pad.

CREWELWORK COVER DESIGN AND STITCH CHART

Key to DMC Medici wools used: 1 skein each of:
pale yellow 8027
crimson 8102
red 8103
orange 8129
pale pink 8139
deep blue 8203
pale blue 8210
light yellow 8326
pale mustard 8327
bright green 8341
deep bright green 8401
beige 8501
pale green 8567
khaki 8610
pink 8817
very pale green 8871
grey blue 8932
deep yellow 8941
Blanc white
All wool used is DMC Medici

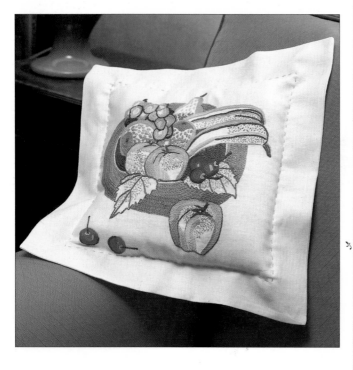

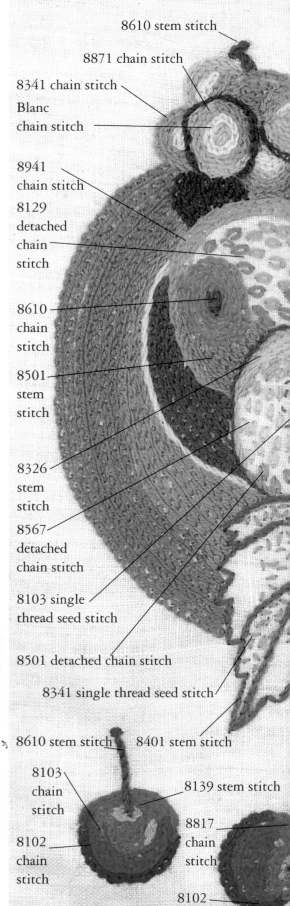

8610 stem stitch

8871 chain stitch

8341 chain stitch

Blanc
chain stitch

8941
chain stitch

8129
detached
chain
stitch

8610
chain
stitch

8501
stem
stitch

8326
stem
stitch

8567
detached
chain stitch

8103 single
thread seed stitch

8501 detached chain stitch

8341 single thread seed stitch

8610 stem stitch   8401 stem stitch

8103
chain
stitch

8139 stem stitch

8817
chain
stitch

8102
chain
stitch

8102

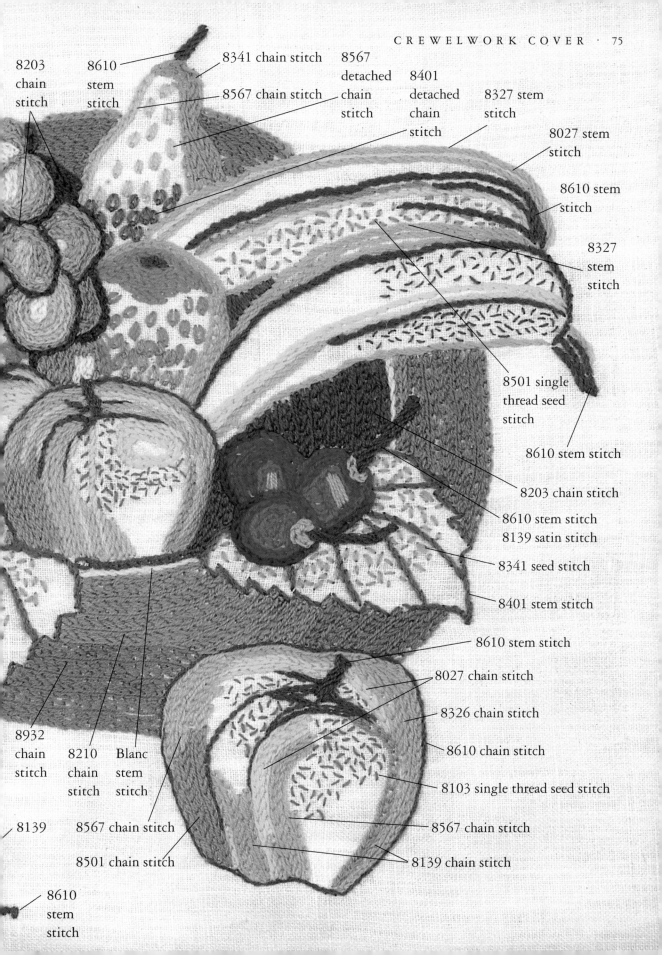

8203 chain stitch

8610 stem stitch

8341 chain stitch

8567 chain stitch

8567 detached chain stitch

8401 detached chain stitch

8327 stem stitch

8027 stem stitch

8610 stem stitch

8327 stem stitch

8501 single thread seed stitch

8610 stem stitch

8203 chain stitch

8610 stem stitch

8139 satin stitch

8341 seed stitch

8401 stem stitch

8610 stem stitch

8027 chain stitch

8326 chain stitch

8610 chain stitch

8103 single thread seed stitch

8932 chain stitch

8210 chain stitch

Blanc stem stitch

8139

8567 chain stitch

8501 chain stitch

8567 chain stitch

8139 chain stitch

8610 stem stitch

Needlepoint cover

Needlepoint is a hardwearing embroidery worked in wool over a canvas or sturdy even-weave base. As the background is woven into even squares each stitch is worked over one or more intersections, completely covering the background. The result is a firm fabric that is ideal for soft furnishings such as cushions and seat covers.

Before you begin, identify the different yarn shades and attach a small length of each one to the appropriate colour on the chart for easy reference.

MATERIALS: 50cm (20in) square of ten mesh canvas, 50cm (20in) square of backing fabric, masking tape, tapestry frame, Paterna Persian yarn in the colours and amounts shown on chart (see pages 78–79), tapestry needle, blotting paper and clean, soft board and drawing pins (optional), 40cm (16in) square cushion pad, sewing thread to match backing fabric, tacking thread, tape measure, scissors and pins

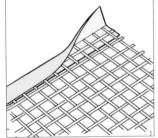

1 To prevent canvas edges fraying, fold masking tape over them, leaving a border of about 7.5cm (3in) around the design. Using yarn in a contrasting colour, tack across the centre of the canvas both ways to find the centre. These stitches can also be used as guidelines (you could add further guidelines at ten-hole intervals).

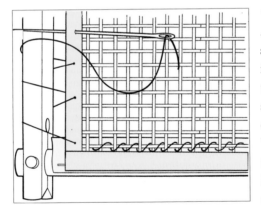

2 To make it easier to work, fit the canvas into a tapestry frame as follows. Mark the centre of the frame's webbing strips. Match these to the centre of the canvas and oversew the top and base edges of the canvas to the webbing strips. Wind any surplus canvas round the rollers until the canvas is taut, then lace the side edges of canvas round the side laths of the frame.

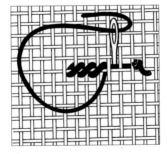

3 The wool yarn is made up of three strands – use all of them in your needle. Work with a 45cm (18in) length of yarn. To begin, knot the end of the yarn and take it through the canvas from front to back, about 2cm (¾in) in front of the starting point. Bring the needle up at the first stitch and work the first few stitches over the end of the yarn to fasten it neatly in place on the reverse side. When you reach the knot, snip it off. Start any subsequent lengths by sliding the needle under a few stitches on the reverse side. To end a length, slide the needle under a few stitches on the reverse and trim closely.

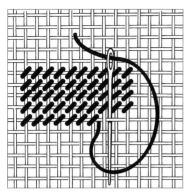

4 Work the design in half cross stitch (see Embroidery Stitches, pages 88–89). Each square of the chart represents one half cross stitch worked on the canvas. Each stitch is worked over one canvas thread intersection. Ensure that all the stitches slope in the same direction. Make each stitch in two movements up through the canvas and back down. Keep your right hand below the canvas to guide the needle and the left hand above it, to feed the needle into the holes.

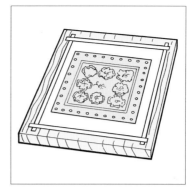

5 When the design is complete, it may need to be 'blocked' to return the canvas to its original size. On a sheet of blotting paper, mark out the original size of the tapestry. Cover a clean, soft board with the blotting paper. Gently wet the back of the canvas with a fine spray of water. Place the canvas face down on the board and, using rust-proof tacks or drawing pins, pin the work down, spacing the pins approximately 2.5cm (1in) apart. Pull the canvas gently into shape, adjusting the pins until you are satisfied that it is correct. Leave to dry at room temperature and away from direct sunlight.

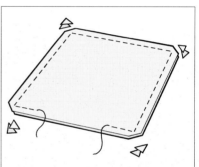

6 Cut out the canvas piece, leaving 2.5cm (1in) of unworked canvas on all the edges. Using this as a guide, cut out a piece of backing fabric to the same size. Place fabric to canvas with right sides facing. Pin, tack and stitch all round, leaving an opening centrally in the base edge. Trim and turn right side out. Insert cushion pad and close opening.

Key to Paterna Persian yarns used:

- 6 skeins of dark hyacinth blue 340
- 4 skeins of mid hyacinth blue 342
- 3 skeins of dark blue 540
- 2 skeins of royal blue 542
- 1 skein of light blue 545
- 2 skeins of navy blue 571
- 9 skeins of cream 764
- 2 skeins of pale orange 770
- 2 skeins of yellow 771
- 4 skeins of pale yellow 773
- 2 skeins of orange 813

WORKING FROM A CHART

Each square on a needlepoint chart represents one stitch worked over one canvas intersection. The colour of the yarn is shown by a similar painted colour in each square. As a general rule, begin in the middle and work outwards, or stitch the main motifs first and then fill in the background.

Sewing Techniques

In this chapter we show you all you need to know to make up successful cushions. First, collect the basic sewing equipment. If you sew on a fairly regular basis, you will probably already have most of the things you require in your sewing basket. The same applies for the basic techniques – if you can thread a needle and stitch a straight seam, then you can make up the majority of the cushions in this book.

To help you with the more elaborate designs, simple embroidery and needlepoint techniques are explained in detail so it's really easy for you to create stunning hand-worked pieces that can be turned into unique cushions. Finally, handy reference pages include patterns for some of the cushion styles featured in the book, a useful glossary of terms, and a few pointers on basic cushion care.

Essential sewing equipment

Check through this listing and you may well be surprised by just how much sewing equipment you already have. None of these items are complicated to use or expensive, and they will leave you well-prepared to tackle almost any kind of cushion you can think of.

MEASURING

Tape measure

Choose a non-stretch tape with metal ends. Ideally, it should have both metric and imperial measurements featured on both sides.

MARKING

Tailors' chalk

This is available in different colours so you can mark most fabric shades. The chalk brushes away after stitching. Keep the chalk sharp, so it will mark accurate lines.

CUTTING

Cutting out scissors

These large, strong scissors have handles that bend away from the blades. This means that you can cut material flat on the table, without lifting it up, which prevents distortion when cutting out fabric pieces.

General sewing scissors

Use these for trimming seams and threads. Again, choose a standard size with 15cm (6in) long blades.

Pinking shears

These scissors give a zigzag edge and are used for neatening seam allowances. Do not use them for cutting out fabric pieces, as they won't provide an accurate edge.

Needlework scissors

The sharp points of these blades are useful for snipping into sharp corners.

SEWING

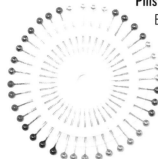

Pins

Before you begin to sew, check that the pins are sharp and discard blunt or damaged pins as they will snag the fabric. Glass-headed pins are useful when working with pile or open-weave fabrics (you can also spot them on the floor!)

Needles

Keep a good range of needle types and sizes in your work-box to cover all kinds of fabrics and trims. The most useful are:-

Sharps: long needles used for tacking and gathering.

Betweens: small, sharp needles used for hand-sewing.

Ball-point needles: used on knitted fabric to prevent snagging.

Bodkins: short, blunt needles used for threading cord and elastic through casings.

SEWING MACHINES

A sewing machine is a must for the committed home sewer. First, decide what type of sewing you want to do. Machines come in a wide range of different models and almost all models do a basic lockstitch and a zigzag stitch for neatening edges and working buttonholes. More expensive machines offer embroidery

stitches. Select needles to match your fabric – from number 70 for fine fabrics to 110 for thicker ones.

PRESSING

You'll need a good, clean, dry or steam iron, plus a clean ironing board. Keep a clean cloth for pressing delicate fabrics and for when you need extra steam on hard-to-press creases in natural fabrics.

THE RIGHT THREAD FOR THE JOB

Cotton thread
Smooth, strong thread with a slight sheen. Use this on cotton fabric.

Mercerised cotton thread
A treated cotton thread available in a huge range of colours.

Polyester thread
All-purpose thread, suitable for a variety of fabrics.

Cotton-wrapped polyester
The polyester provides strength while the cotton provides smoothness and lustre.

Silk thread
Use for stitching silk and hand-tacking fine fabrics (as it leaves no marks).

Tacking thread
Loosely twisted cotton thread, easy to break and so quick to remove from fabrics.

Buttonhole twist
Use for topstitching as well as buttonholes. Available in synthetic or silk.

Seams and stitching

Knowing how to make seams properly forms the nuts-and-bolts of successful sewing, whatever you are creating. It is especially important to have strong, neat seams on cushions, as they are often highly visible and can take quite a lot of wear and tear.

PLAIN FLAT SEAM

1 Place the two pieces of fabric with right sides together and raw edges matching. Pin together across the seamline, placing pins approximately 8cm (3in) apart, as shown. Tack along the seamline.

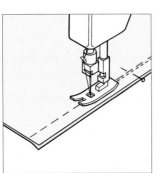

2 Position the sewing machine foot so the point of the needle is aligned with the seamline, approximately 1.25cm (½in) away from the end of the seam. Work stitches in reverse to the fabric edge, then stitch forward down the complete seam. At the end of the seam, work stitches in reverse for approximately 1.25cm (½in).

3 Remove the fabric from the machine and trim off thread ends. Press the seam as it has been stitched, then press the seam open. To achieve a good seamline, press over a seam roller.

STITCHING ROUND CORNERS

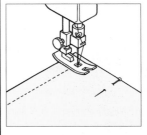

1 Form neat corners, stitch along the seamline up to the corner, with the needle in the fabric. Raise the presser foot and pivot the fabric until the needle is in line with the next seamline.

2 Lower the presser foot and continue along the seamline. On heavy fabrics it may be necessary to work stitches across the corner point, as shown.

STITCHING CURVED SEAMS

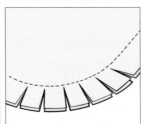

1 Stitch curved seams in the usual way. On outward curves, snip into the seam allowance so that the fabric can spread out.

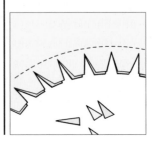

2 On inward curves, cut out small notches from the seam allowance so that, when the seam is pressed flat, the allowance can overlap.

FRENCH SEAM

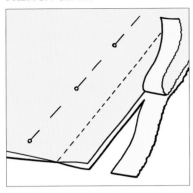

1 Place fabric pieces with wrong sides together. Pin, tack and stitch, taking 5mm (¼in) allowance. Trim down the allowance to 3mm (⅛in).

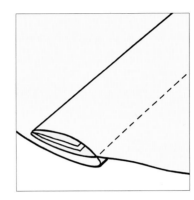

2 Refold the fabric with right sides together, pressing the seam so that it lies exactly along the edge. Pin, tack and stitch 1cm (⅜in) from the seamed edge.

FLAT FELL SEAM

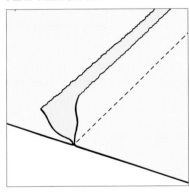

1 Place the two fabric pieces with right sides together and raw edges matching. Pin, tack and stitch, following the seamline. Press the seam open and then to one side.

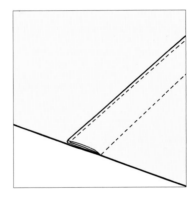

2 Trim inner seam allowance to just under half width. Fold the top seam allowance over the inner seam allowance, then press the seam. Pin, tack and edgestitch along the folded edge.

PIPED SEAM

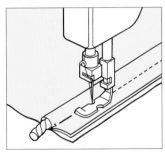

1 Make up a length of covered piping cord in the usual way. Lay the piping cord along the seamline of the first fabric piece, with the cord facing inwards and raw edges matching the raw fabric edges; pin and tack in place. Using a piping foot on the machine, stitch down the seamline.

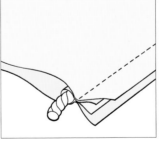

2 Place the second fabric piece against the first piece, right sides together, sandwiching the piping in between and matching raw edges. Pin, tack and stitch down the seamline again, using the previous stitching line as a guide.

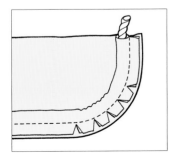

3 On curved seams, snip into the piping allowance at regular intervals all round the curved edge.

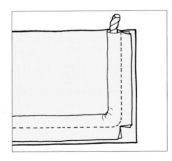

4 At sharp corners, snip into the piping allowance from the corner point up to the stitching line, to help spread the fabric out at the corner.

Hand-stitching

The following are the main hand-stitched techniques you'll need in order to tackle a full range of cushions.

GATHERING FABRIC BY HAND

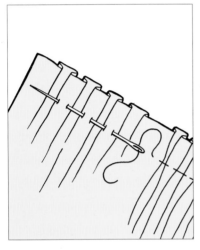

1 Work from the right side, with thread approximately 20cm (8in) longer than the length to be gathered. Work a few running stitches at a time, before pulling the thread through the fabric.

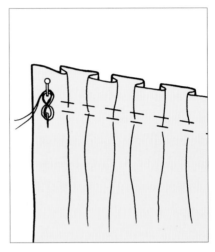

2 Work a second row of running stitch in the same way, 5mm (¼in) above the first row. Pull up both gathering threads together to form even gathers.

BACKSTITCH

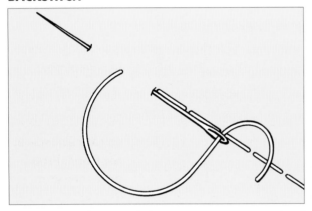

Work from right to left, beginning with a couple of stitches worked on the spot. Bring the threaded needle up through the fabric and then take it back down about half a stitch's length behind the point where the thread emerged. Now bring the needle up the same distance in front of this point. Continue in this way to the end of the seam. End with a couple of backstitches worked on the spot.

FEATHER STITCH

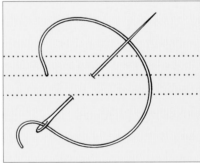

1 Make the stitch by taking the needle diagonally through the fabric left to right and below the thread, making a loop.

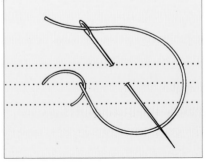

2 Take the needle through the fabric again, working right to left and making a loop. Continue alternating stitches.

HERRINGBONE STITCH

A strong stitch used for hems, holding raw edges, and joining lengths of wadding. Work from left to right, with the needle pointing towards the left. Secure the thread with a couple of backstitches. Take a stitch from right to left in one fabric then take the needle up across the edge and take another stitch from right to left in the second. Continue, forming evenly spaced crossed stitches.

RUNNING STITCH

Use this for gathering fabric. Begin with a couple of backstitches, then work from right to left, weaving the needle in and out of the fabric and taking small, evenly spaced stitches.

SLIPSTITCH

An almost invisible stitch used to hold two folded edges together – for example, across a cushion opening. Work from right to left. Begin with a knot and secure inside the fold of the hem. Bring the thread out of one folded edge and slide inside the opposite folded edge. Come out of this fold and repeat.

STABSTITCH

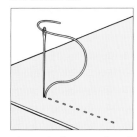

A useful stitch to hold two pieces of fabric together with almost invisible stitches, such as for appliqué. Work from right to left with the needle in a vertical position, taking tiny stitches on the right side of the fabric. On the wrong side the stitches will be slightly longer.

TACKING

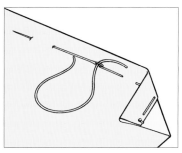

Work with a single or double thread and begin with a knot. Work through the fabric, making stitches and gaps approximately 1–2cm (⅜-¾in) long. At the opposite end, take one backstitch and trim off the thread. To remove tacking stitches, simply snip off the knot and pull the thread out of the fabric.

DIAGONAL TACKING

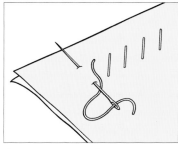

This is the best way to hold two slippery fabrics together or to secure pleats or layers of wadding to a fabric. With the needle pointing from right to left, take horizontal stitches through the fabric, forming rows of slanting stitches. Work vertically or horizontally across the fabric.

SLIP-TACKING (LADDER STITCH)

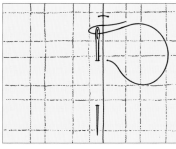

Use this to match two patterned pieces of fabric together. The tacking is worked on the right side of the fabric. Press under one seam allowance and pin over the opposite seam allowance, exactly matching the pattern design. Working from the right side, take a 1.5cm (⅝in) long stitch through the folded edge. Bring out the needle, take it vertically across the seamline and slide it under the flat fabric for 1.5cm (⅝in). Continue stitching ladder stitches across the join in this way. When the seam is complete, simply fold the fabric with right sides together and stitch along the seamline.

Embroidery stitches

Illustrated here are all the embroidery and needlepoint stitches you will need to make the hand-worked cushion covers in this book (see pages 72–79). With a little imagination, it is easy to create attractive covers of your own design.

CHAINSTITCH

This can be stitched in closely worked rows to cover areas of a design.

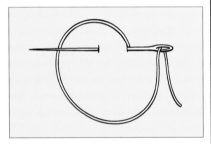

1 Bring the needle out of the fabric and take a stitch through the fabric from the original point.

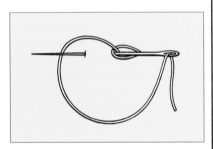

2 Pull through the fabric over the working thread, forming a loop.

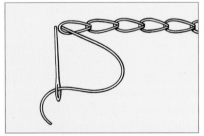

3 To finish, make a small stitch over the last chain in the row.

DETACHED CHAINSTITCH (LAZY DAISY STITCH)

This stitch is the same as chainstitch but is worked as separate stitches.

1 Form a loop in exactly the same way as chainstitch.

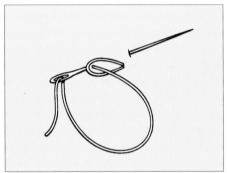

2 Once the chain is formed, take a small backstitch over the end then take the needle under the fabric to the position for the next stitch.

SATIN STITCH

This fills in an area with long, straight stitches.

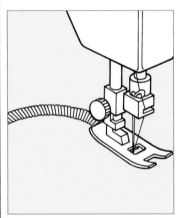

By machine: set the zig zag button on your machine to make wide, closely worked stitches.

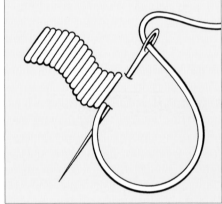

By hand: using an embroidery needle make long, straight stitches close together, keeping the thread flat and the stitches even.

SEED STITCH

Use in groups or scattered all over a design.

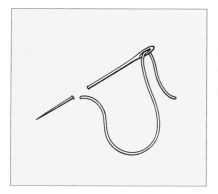

1 Bring the needle out of the fabric and take a tiny back stitch.

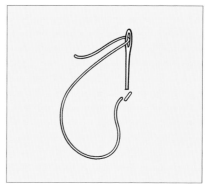

2 Repeat, placing two stitches side by side, before moving on to the position of the next stitch.

STEMSTITCH

Stemstitch is usually used to outline areas of a design. Work from left to right.

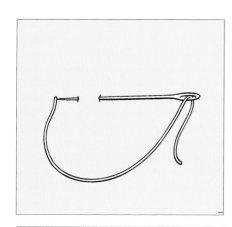

1 Bring the needle out of the fabric and take a backstitch, bringing the needle up again halfway along the first stitch.

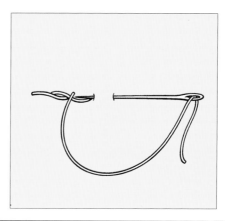

2 Repeat this sequence, keeping the thread below the needle to form neat, overlapping stitches.

HALF CROSS-STITCH

Work this needlepoint stitch in two movements, with the main guiding hand below the canvas and the other hand above the canvas. Work from left to right.

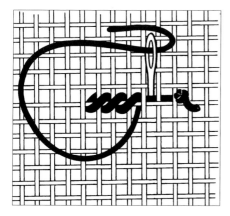

1 Come out of the canvas and take a diagonal stitch from left to right over one intersection, bringing the needle out one hole below.

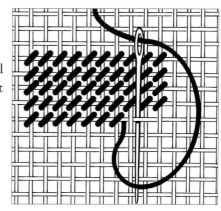

2 Work the second row in reverse, or simply turn the canvas and work back the same way.

Templates

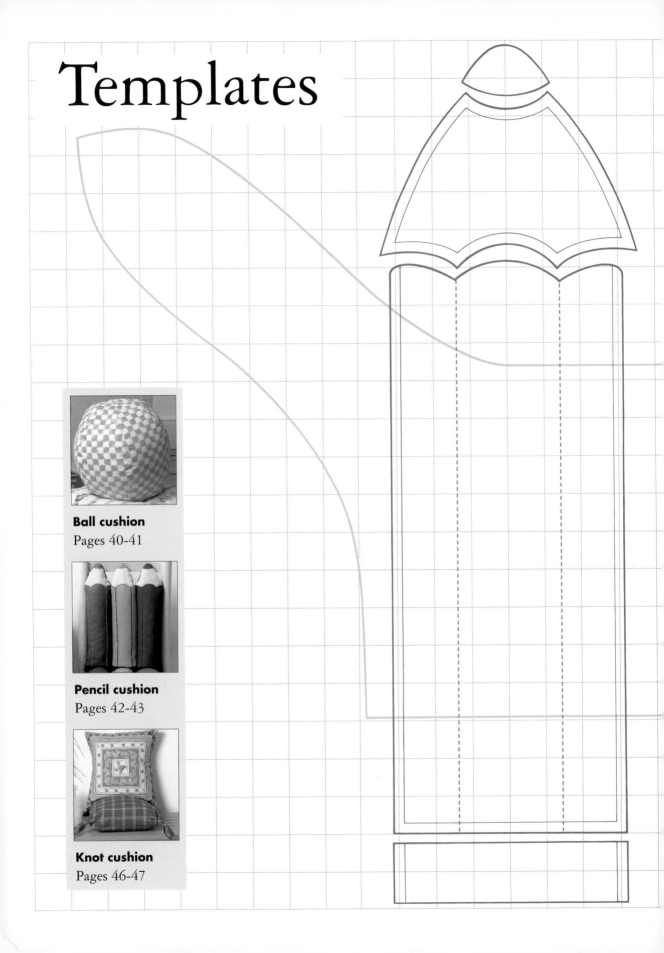

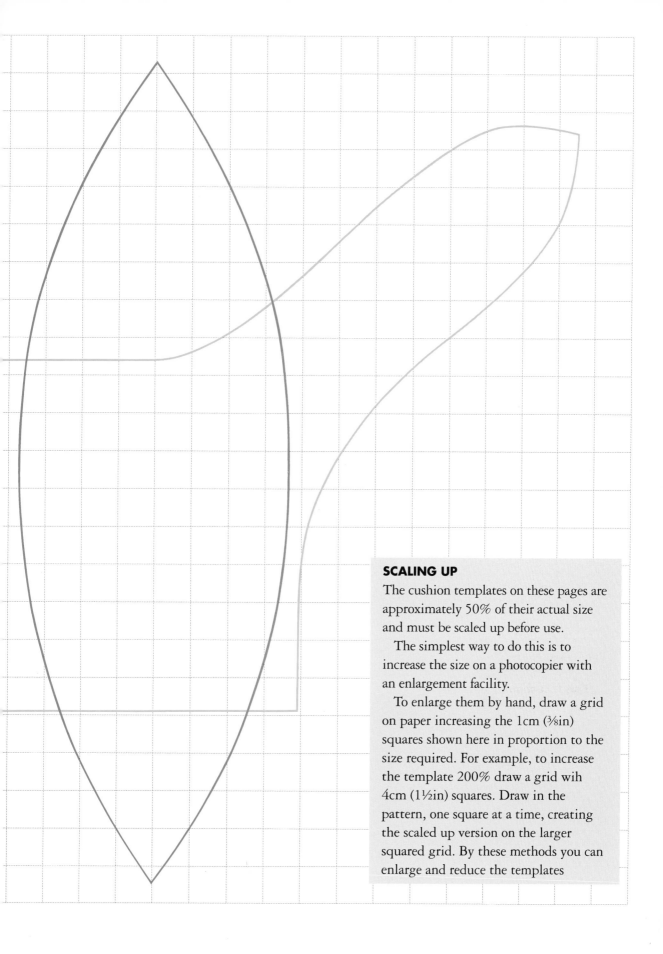

SCALING UP

The cushion templates on these pages are approximately 50% of their actual size and must be scaled up before use.

The simplest way to do this is to increase the size on a photocopier with an enlargement facility.

To enlarge them by hand, draw a grid on paper increasing the 1cm (⅜in) squares shown here in proportion to the size required. For example, to increase the template 200% draw a grid wih 4cm (1½in) squares. Draw in the pattern, one square at a time, creating the scaled up version on the larger squared grid. By these methods you can enlarge and reduce the templates

Glossary

Appliqué
A design created when one fabric or shape is applied to another.

Bias
The diagonal line of fabric formed when the lengthways grain of the fabric is folded to meet the crossways grain of the fabric.

Bias binding
Strip of fabric that is cut along the bias and used to bind curved edges.

Brocade
Distinctive fabric with differently woven areas forming a raised pattern.

Calico
Strong, cheap woven cotton fabric, available unbleached or bleached.

Casing
A channel formed by two parallel rows of stitching.

Crewelwork
Embroidery using wool thread on a fabric background.

Devoré velvet
Velvet fabric chemically treated to 'devour' some of the pile, leaving a pattern.

Embroidery hoop
Two close fitting wooden hoops that holds taut a piece of embroidery while it is worked.

Gathering
A running or machine stitch that is pulled up to regulate the fullness of a piece of fabric.

Grain
The direction in which the fibres run in a length of fabric.

Gusset
Strip of fabric added between a top and bottom piece to give depth.

Mitre
A corner seam that neatly joins two hems at right angles to each other.

Mounting
Two layers of fabric, tacked together and worked as one. Useful with delicate fabric.

Muslin
Fine cotton fabric that can be used as a backing.

Needlepoint
Wool or yarn embroidery worked over a sturdy canvas or even-weave fabric.

Piping
Piping is a folded strip of fabric, inserted into a seam as an edging. It can be flat or form a covering for piping cord.

Pivot
To create a sharp corner by leaving the needle in the fabric and turning the fabric.

Poplin

Popular hard-wearing cotton fabric with a slight sheen.

Pre-shrinking

Shrinking fabric and trimmings to prevent shrinkage after they have been made up.

Quilting

A decorative method of joining two pieces of fabric with a wadded centre.

Seam allowance

The amount of fabric allowed for stitching seams – generally 1.5cm (⅝in).

Seamline

The line designated for stitching the seam.

Selvedge

The non-fraying, tightly-woven edge running down both side edges of a length of fabric.

Tapestry frame

Wooden frame, used to hold a piece of canvas or fabric taut, while embroidering.

Tension

The balance and tightness of the needle and bobbin threads on a sewing machine that combine to create the perfect stitch.

Thread count

The number of threads per cm (inch) in the warp and weft threads of canvas or embroidery fabrics.

Tucks

Narrow stitch fold of fabric which provide a decorative feature.

Wadding

Bonded fabric, in various thicknesses, used to add depth and warmth to another fabric.

Zigzag stitch

Machine stitch used to neaten seams and as a decorative stitch.

CUSHION CARE

- Shake out and air pads regularly.
- Wash feather pads in warm, sudsy water and rinse well. Keep shaking as they dry. Wash synthetic-filled pads by hand or machine and tumble dry. Do not dry clean pads – the filling can absorb toxic cleaning fluid fumes. Foam pads can be washed gently in warm, sudsy water. Rinse, squeeze well and dry in a warm place, away from direct heat to avoid fumes from the foam.
- Treat any stains as they occur and then wash the cover.
- When washing covers, close zips and fastenings.
- Press covers while slightly damp to iron out any creases.
- Dry clean any covers whose fibre content you are unsure of.

Index

Cushions

Credits and acknowledgements.

The author and publishers would like to thank the following for their assistance in producing this book:

Crewelwork cushion designed by Anna Griffiths, Needlepoint cushion designed by Betty Barnden for Paterna, and ribbons by Panda, woven by Selectus Ltd. With special thanks to Penny Hill and Beryl Miller. Location photography with the kind permission of Di Hooley and Steven Ferdinando and for the generous provision of fabric, Anna French Ltd: pages 14, 22, 24, 26, 32, 40; Crowson Fabrics Ltd: pages 16, 18, 20, 28, 30, 46, 56, 58, 62.

Photographic Credits
Key: t – top, b – bottom, l – left, r – right
Elizabeth Whiting & Associates: all on p6, *l* x2 on p7, x2 on p8, *bl* on p9, x2 on p10 /
Anna French Ltd: *tr* on p7, *t* on p9 / Crowson Fabrics: *br* on p7

Written by: Hilary More

Managing editor: Felicity Jackson
Project editor: Finny Fox-Davies
Editor: Ann Kay

Art director: Graham Webb
Design: Design Section
Photography: George Wright
Picture research: Nell Hunter
Illustrator: Geoff Denny Associates

Production
controller: Louise McIntyre

Published by Haynes Publishing
Sparkford, Nr Yeovil, Somerset BA22 7JJ

British Library Cataloguing-in-Publication Data:
A catalogue record of this book is available from the British Library

ISBN 1 85960 316 5

Printed in France by
Imprimerie Pollina S.A.

Hilary More has asserted her right to be identified as the author of this work

First published 1998